THE LONDON MINI AND MIDI BUS TYPES

THE LONDON MINI AND MIDI BUS TYPES

DAVID BEDDALL

PEN & SWORD
TRANSPORT

AN IMPRINT OF PEN & SWORD BOOKS LTD.
YORKSHIRE – PHILADELPHIA

First published in Great Britain in 2024 by
Pen and Sword Transport
An imprint of
Pen & Sword Books Ltd.
Yorkshire - Philadelphia

Copyright © David Beddall, 2024

ISBN 978 1 39909 526 6

The right of David Beddall to be identified as author of this work has been asserted by him in accordance with the Copyright, Designs and Patents Act 1988.

A CIP catalogue record for this book is available from the British Library.

Typeset by SJmagic DESIGN SERVICES, India.

Printed and bound by Printworks Global Ltd, London/Hong Kong.

Pen & Sword Books Ltd. incorporates the imprints of Pen & Sword Books: After the Battle, Archaeology, Atlas, Aviation, Battleground, Discovery, Family History, History, Maritime, Military, Politics, Select, Transport, True Crime, Fiction, Frontline Books, Leo Cooper, Praetorian Press, Seaforth Publishing, Wharncliffe and White Owl.

For a complete list of Pen & Sword titles please contact

PEN & SWORD BOOKS LIMITED
George House, Units 12 & 13, Beevor Street, Off Pontefract Road,
Barnsley, South Yorkshire, S71 1HN, England
E-mail: enquiries@pen-and-sword.co.uk
Website: www.pen-and-sword.co.uk

or

PEN AND SWORD BOOKS
1950 Lawrence Rd, Havertown, PA 19083, USA
E-mail: uspen-and-sword@casematepublishers.com
Website: www.penandswordbooks.com

CONTENTS

INTRODUCTION

The term minibus usually refers to a small bus that seats no more than twenty-five passengers. They were usually available as both vans and buses. A midibus is traditionally a bus that measures no more than 10.0m in length, although some of the more modern types can push this length up to 11.0m. For the purpose of this book, the majority of types under the midibus title will not exceed the 10.0m length.

The first small buses to operate in the London area did so in the 1930s, when many were taken into stock by the London Passenger Transport Board from London General and various independent operators. By 1940, these had mostly disappeared in favour of larger buses. There were, of course, some exceptions such as the Leyland Cub and the Guy Special GS-class, the history of the latter type being too complex to include in this book. The Leyland Cub itself was the first new small bus to be purchased by London Transport, catering for London Transport's smaller bus requirements in both the Central and Country areas. The GS-class was used to negotiate the narrow country lanes in Hertfordshire. London Transport adopted a big bus policy after the war, with many of the small buses being withdrawn.

Ford Transit minibuses were introduced in the 1970s, allowing buses to serve previously unserved areas of London. These sixteen-seater minibuses were the first to gain the 'bread van' nickname, but were not the last, this being applied to a number of types introduced in the late 1980s, early 1990s. The Ford Transit was used on four routes in the Bromley, Enfield, Potters Bar and Stockwell areas of London.

In the mid-1980s, London Buses began to reverse its big-bus policy in favour of small, more cost effective mini and midibuses. A large number of these vehicles were purchased, with various Iveco and Mercedes-Benz models entering service, along with the MCW and Optare MetroRiders. A number of new routes were introduced during this time, entering housing estates that had previously been unserved by buses. The introduction of these new routes and smaller buses was a success, with many suffering capacity issues, causing the introduction of the larger Dennis Dart and later Dennis Dart SLF models, these eventually replacing the majority of the midibuses, these two models being midibuses themselves.

The introduction of the shorter Dennis Dart MPD, measuring 8.8m, saw the need for other types diminish as the MPD provided the majority of London's smaller bus needs. However, a handful of routes continued to be operated by small midibuses. In the low-floor era, the other midibus needs were mostly met by the Optare Solo and Solo SR models. A handful of smaller Mercedes-Benz Sprinters were also used where needed.

2004 saw the introduction of the Enviro 200 model, this eventually replacing the Dennis Dart SLF, and again a short version was produced and, like the MPD, they also provided the solution for the smaller bus needs in the capital.

The aim of this book is to give you an insight into the mini and midibus operations in London, starting with a look at the small buses inherited by London Transport. We then move on and look at the introduction of the Ford Transit, along with the Bristol LH and LHS models in the 1970s, these also coming under the definition of a midibus. We then move on to the various mini and midibus types introduced in the 1980s and 1990s, being completed by the newer low-floor era midibuses introduced in the 2000s and 2010s.

David Beddall
Rushden, 2023

ACKNOWLEDGEMENTS

I would like to say a big thank you to my wife Helen for her support during the production of this book. A big thank you also goes to Liam Farrer-Beddall for taking the time to proofread the draft and for allowing me access to his photo archive. I would also like to thank Ian Armstrong, Mike Harris, S.J. Butler, Matthew Wharmby, Bill Young, Glyn Matthews, Michael Whadman, Steve Maskell, the late Jeff Lloyd and Gary Seamarks for allowing me access to their photo archives.

EARLY SMALL BUSES

Over the course of 1933 and 1934 London Transport inherited a number of smaller buses from both the London General Omnibus Company and other independent operators based on the edges of London. This section takes a look at the different types inherited.

Morris Viceroy

London General purchased a Morris Viceroy demonstrator in December 1930, and placed it under the care of East Surrey Traction Company Ltd. This vehicle carried registration mark HA7041. The vehicle was acquired by London Transport, taking rolling stock number MS2 with its new owner.

MS2 (HA7041) was purchased by London General and operated by the East Surrey Traction Company. It was photographed in Amersham under London Transport ownership. *D.W.K. Jones Archive/S.J. Butler Collection*

Twelve one-man operated buses were needed by East Surrey in 1931 for operation on routes in the Darneth and Woking areas of Surrey. It was at this time that East Surrey had acquired the operations of the Darneth Bus Company and Woking & District. Six 20-seat Morris Viceroys were purchased by East Surrey and worked alongside a fleet of six Commer Invaders seating eighteen. The Morris saloons were registered PL6461 to PL6466, with the first four being purchased by London General and operated on their behalf by East Surrey, whilst the last two members of the batch were owned by East Surrey themselves. They arrived between May and July 1931, carrying 20-seat Weymann bodywork. In April 1932, the East Surrey operation was acquired by London General Country Services Ltd.

A pair of 20-seater Harrington bodied Morris Viceroy coaches registered PL6459 and PL6460 arrived in July 1931. They were put to use on private hire work by East Surrey, who briefly owned the pair before they passed to the ownership of Green Line Coaches Ltd in April 1932.

Both the buses and coaches passed to the ownership of the London Passenger Transport Board in July 1933. It was at this time that they gained rolling stock numbers MS4 to MS11. The two coaches were allocated to the private hire fleet, with MS10 being allocated to Old Kent Road, whilst Brixton took stock of MS11.

In addition to these, two other Morris Viceroys were acquired from independent operators. AKJ872, a Duple bodied Viceroy, was acquired in January 1934 from Grey Motor Coach Services of Longfield. New to this operator in 1933, it was given fleet number MS1, and saw service from Guildford on route 448. It lasted with London Transport until June 1938 when it was sold.

MS9 (PL6466) was new to East Surrey. It is seen in Uxbridge whilst heading to Tring on route 397. *D.W.K. Jones Archive/ S.J. Butler Collection*

The other Viceroy was new to Lewis Omnibus Co. of Watford in 1932, again carrying Duple bodywork. Registered JH2585, this vehicle entered the London Transport fleet in October 1933, becoming MS3 in 1935. It lasted another year before leaving the fleet in April 1936. By 1936 these vehicles, with the exception of MS3 which had been withdrawn by this time, were allocated to Amersham where they took over a number of small bus routes, replacing Dennis saloons. They remained there until October 1937, when they were replaced by Leyland Cubs, which themselves had been replaced by AEC Regals.

The Viceroy was not the only Morris chassis to be operated by London Transport, a number of other small Morris saloons were acquired from independent operators in the Windsor and Slough areas. Most of the vehicles concerned gained a new livery of green and black, operating until 1936. A 14-seater Morris R, complete with Buckingham bodywork was acquired from London General Country Services in July 1933. Carrying registration mark UU5009, this vehicle was new to the Great Western Railway in 1931, passing to London General in April 1932. It operated in the Watford area. It was followed in January 1934 by PF1198. This was a Morris 1 ton saloon, new to H.T. Molyneaux of Bletchingley in 1926. In February 1934, RX3459 was acquired from the Nippy Bus Service of Windsor. The latter operator acquired this vehicle from W.F. Clatworthy of Windsor in March 1933. This 14-seat Morris Z6 was used by London Transport on local services in the Windsor area.

A Reall bodied Morris Commercial TX saloon from Cream Service of Slough, registered RX5232, arrived in March 1934; this vehicle was new to Crescent Coaches of Windsor in 1929 and could seat eighteen. Another two Morris Commercial TX saloons, again with Reall bodywork, were also acquired at the same time from Cream Service, Slough. RX5634 was a 14-seater whilst RX9603 had a higher seating capacity of twenty.

In December 1929, Hewins Garage of Maidenhead purchased a 20-seat Duple bodied Morris saloon registered RX5736. It was acquired by F.C. Owen of Slough in February 1930, who down seated it to a 14-seater in July 1931. London Transport acquired the vehicle in July 1935. The final pair of small Morris saloons came in the form of the 30cwt model, seating fourteen. KX3813 and KX3814 were new to Borough Bus of Windsor in 1929 and were taken into stock by London Transport in October 1935.

A slightly larger Morris saloon was acquired in November 1934 from Imperial Bus Service of Romford. VX9932 was an example of the Morris Commercial Dictator model which carried a 26-seat Metcalfe body. It took up rolling stock number M50 for use in the Central Area but was not used by London Transport.

Thornycroft

London Transport inherited a number of Thornycroft buses from a handful of independent operators but did not purchase any new versions themselves. A handful of longer Thornycroft BCs and Cygnets were acquired from the Great Western Railway, Woking & District or People's of Ware. Alongside these vehicles, sixteen Thornycroft 'Nippy' 20-seater buses were acquired from various sources. These small buses were based on either the A12 or A2L chassis.

Nine of these saloons were acquired from People's Motor Service of Ware, carrying Thurgood bodywork. Three of these saloons were Thornycroft A12s, which carried registration marks JH492, JH1586 and JH2054. Taken into stock by London Transport in December 1933, they were numbered NY1 to NY3 in 1935. The other six were based on the A2L chassis. Registered UR7141/2, 7353, 7968 and 9176, they continued the fleet number sequence as NY4 to NY9. When operated by People's of Ware, the NY-class were used on rural services in the Hertford and Ware areas of Hertfordshire. Under the control of London Transport, the majority transferred to Addlestone for further country work. NY8 found itself operating from Northfleet garage. Withdrawal of the type took place between 1936 and 1938.

Five Thornycroft A2Ls preceded the batch acquired from People's of Ware. July 1933 saw the small batch acquired from London General Country Services. These Thornycroft A2Ls were new to Woking and District in 1929, passing to East Surrey Motor Traction in January 1931. Four carried bodywork constructed by Challands Ross, these carrying registration marks PG1099, PG2018, PG3236 and PG4226. The fifth member of the batch was bodied by Wilton and was registered VB4550. London General acquired the batch in January 1932. These vehicles were transferred out of the Woking area, some going to Dunton Green, where they were put to use on services in the Knockholt area, and some moved to Chelsham. These did not last as long as the batch previously mentioned, being sold between January and April 1936, their place being taken by the Leyland Cub.

It wasn't until October 1939 that the final pair of small Thornycrofts was acquired by London Transport, when the operations of West Kent Motors were acquired by the concern. At this time, the latter Company was operating a Thornycroft A2L which was new to West Kent in April 1928, and a Thornycroft Dainty, new in January 1938. The A2L was registered KO9092 and carried bodywork manufactured by Vincent. The Dainty was registered EKP140 and carried Thurgood bodywork. Both were used in service in the Sevenoaks area of Kent, with the latter vehicle being used on private

JH1586 was one of three Thornycroft A12s new to People's of Ware. It was allocated fleet number NY2 with London Transport. *D.W.K. Jones Archive/ S.J. Butler Collection*

hire work as well as on the route between Sevenoaks and Fawke Common. They were soon disposed of by London Transport without seeing further service.

These small buses proved to be popular with London Transport, and it was their original intention to order a new batch of the type for 1934 delivery. However, the order was altered to the Leyland Cub, the first of which arrived in 1935.

Chevrolet

The name Chevrolet was used by General Motors for the production of small bus chassis' between the late 1920s and 1931, when the UK name was rebranded as Bedford. The first model arrived in 1927 named the LM, this being replaced by the LP in 1928. The 1929 and 1930 models were named the LQ. The final model to be made under the Chevrolet name was the U, constructed over the course of 1930 and 1931, before giving way to the Bedford BD-class. A total of thirty-six Chevrolets were acquired by London Transport through various take overs of independent operators in 1933 and 1934. Many were withdrawn immediately, with others having a brief spell in service.

Five of these were Chevrolet LMs, the first of which originated with People's Bus of Ware, carrying a 14-seat Thurgood body. RO8517 was acquired by London Transport in December 1933, being withdrawn less than a year later in October 1934. The second LM model was registered UC6438. New to Carr & Hollings of Hemel Hempstead in

UR9176 was a Thornycroft A2L saloon, again new to People's of Ware. It was added to the London Transport fleet in December 1933, taking fleet number NY9 at this time. *D.W.K. Jones Archive/S.J. Butler Collection*

1928, it passed to Pioneer of Aspley End in 1931 before entering the London Transport fleet in January 1934. Next came PH6509, another 14-seater saloon. It was acquired in March 1934 from A.R. Rudall of Guildford. The final pair were acquired from Romford-based operators. TW8532 was new to Romford & District in 1927. This vehicle carried a 14-seat Metcalfe body and was acquired by London Transport in July 1934, surviving with them until July 1935. The second came from Imperial Bus Services of Romford. This was another 14-seater saloon, this time carrying Thurgood bodywork. Registered YU9022, it was acquired by London Transport in November 1934, and like TW8532, it was withdrawn in July 1935. These were the only Chevrolet LMs to gain rolling stock numbers, these being CH4 and CH5 respectively.

Just two Chevrolet LPs were acquired. The first was registered KX1580 and originated with the Amersham & District company, who gave it fleet number 5. It was new to Amersham in 1928 carrying a 14-seat Willmott body, passing to London Transport in November 1933, leaving the fleet in April 1934. The second LP was registered KX1343 and was new to A.H. Lucas of Slough. This vehicle carried a Hoyal body, also seating fourteen. It lasted slightly longer than KX1580, being sold in September 1934.

The largest intake of Chevrolets came in the form of fifteen LQ models, acquired by London Transport between July 1933 and August 1936. The first was acquired from London General Country Services registered UR3273. This vehicle was new to A.E. Gilbert of Essendon in May 1929, and was sold by London Transport in May 1935. The second LQ arrived in August 1933 from Barton of Watford. New in 1930, this 20-seater carried registration mark GC5531. It remained with London Transport for just over a year before being sold. UV9957, a 16-seat Chevrolet LQ, moved from Y.S. Coaches of Watford in August 1933. Like GC5531, UV9957 only lasted until September 1934 before leaving the fleet.

Two further Chevrolet LQs arrived in January 1934; both being withdrawn by September of the same year. PK6935 was acquired from R.G. Heywood of Weybridge, dating back to 1929, whilst slightly newer MY6839 arrived from Edward's Motor Service of Rainham, this vehicle being new to them in 1930. A month later, two further LQs were taken into stock from TT Bus Service of Slough. KX4076 was new to this concern, with KX4530 being acquired from Wycombe and District in February 1933. These remained with London Transport until May 1935. PG9110, a dual-doored 14-seat Chevrolet LQ, arrived in February 1934. It was acquired from the Egham Motor Co., being withdrawn in September of the same year. PG7703 followed in March 1934. This was new to the Magnet Omnibus Service of Guildford in 1930, being withdrawn by London Transport in October 1934.

Five Chevrolet LQs were acquired by London Transport in May 1934. The first two were taken into stock from Slough based Bell's Bus Service. Carrying registration marks KX3075 and UW6727, the pair survived until May 1935 and October 1934 respectively. A third was acquired from Clark's Motor Coaches registered UW7614. UR4218 was a 14-seat Thurgood bodied Chevrolet LQ originating with R.J. Allery of Abbots Langley in 1929. In March 1930 it passed to H.G. Biggerstaff of Sarratt before being acquired by London Transport. It lasted in the fleet until May 1935. The final LQ to be acquired in May 1934 came from Speedwell Bus Service of Windsor. Registered KX4534, it was new to F.H. Evans & Sons of High Wycombe in 1930. London Transport withdrew this vehicle in September 1934. The final LQ to be acquired by London Transport was sourced from Regent of Brentwood. VX4074 was a 14-seat Furber bodied LQ and was taken into stock in August 1936. It lasted for less than a year with London Transport, being withdrawn in June 1937.

The final Chevrolet model to be acquired was the Chevrolet U, these totalling eleven. The first pair arrived from Amersham and District in November 1933. They carried registration marks KX6513 and GO9046, the first being withdrawn immediately, whilst the second was withdrawn in October 1934. PL1211 arrived from Reo Omnibus Co. of Addlestone in December 1933, remaining with London Transport until September 1934. A few months passed before the next Chevrolet U was taken into stock by London Transport. HX9677 was new to F. Berry of Slough and carried a 14-seat Reall body. It was withdrawn by its new owner in October 1934. Three further Chevrolet Us arrived with London Transport in April 1934. KX5977 was acquired from F.S. Bowler of Beaconsfield; whilst RX7545 and RX7490 came from A.H. Lucas of Slough. RX7545 carried bodywork constructed by Hoyal, with KX7490 carrying Willmott bodywork. The latter two vehicles were withdrawn in September 1934, whilst KX5977 lasted a month extra, being taken out of service in October. The final quartet arrived in May 1934. RX7617 was new to Speedwell Bus Service of Windsor in 1931, and it was from this operator that it was acquired. The other three were all acquired from Bell's Bus Service of Slough. They carried registration marks GK9584, GJ3757 and HX9676. GJ3757 carried Willowbrook bodywork and was withdrawn straight away by London Transport. HX9676 was bodied by Reall and remained in the fleet for a short while, being withdrawn in October 1934, with GK9584 also being taken out of service at this time.

KX6513 was one of two Chevrolet U saloons to be acquired from Amersham & District. These arrived in November 1933 and only lasted with London Transport for a short while, being withdrawn in 1934. It is seen after withdrawal. *D.W.K. Jones Archive/S.J. Butler Collection*

KX5977 was another Chevrolet U saloon to be taken into stock by London Transport. New to F.S. Bowler of Beaconsfield, it is again photographed after withdrawal by London Transport. *D.W.K. Jones Archive/ S.J. Butler Collection*

Willys-Overland-Crossley Manchester

Out of all of the small buses inherited by London Transport in 1933 and 1934, the Willys-Overland-Crossley would have to be one of the smallest. Gravesend and District of Northfleet was the only operator in the London area to be operating this type, mainly in the form of the Manchester model. The Gravesend business was acquired by London Transport in October 1933. At this time, a solitary 16-seat Overland bus was in use by the company, registered KO3306. It was sold by London Transport in March 1934.

In terms of the Manchester model, Gravesend & District operated both a 2-ton WLV model and the 1.5 ton 6-wheeler, in both bus and coach formats. VX8540 was a Manchester WLV convertible coach, acquired by Gravesend and District from Tilbury Dock Coaches in July 1933. It was used by London Transport for a longer period of time than other members of the type, being converted to a lorry in July 1935 and added to the service fleet.

KR6859 was the first of three 2-ton Manchester models; new to the Company in 1930, it could seat nineteen. In July 1934, this saloon was briefly converted to a petrol lorry, before reverting back to a bus in December. It remained operational with London Transport until April 1936, when it was sold. The other two were 20-seaters, new to Gravesend & District in 1931. These carried registration marks KJ4016 and KJ4191. Both were sold by London Transport in October 1934.

The final pair were both new to Gravesend & District in 1930, registered KR3034 and KR7090. KR3034 lasted until October 1934, at which point it was sold. Like KR6859, in May 1934 KR7090 was converted to a petrol lorry, only to return to use as a bus in December. It was retired from the London Transport fleet in May 1936.

Bean Buses

Nineteen small buses manufactured by Bean were operated on the edges of London. East Surrey purchased a solitary 20-seater Bean in July 1929. Registered RF5806, it later passed to London General Country Services before being taken into stock by London Transport in July 1933.

East Surrey operated four additional Bean saloons, these being inherited from C.H. Hever, who traded as the Darenth Bus Service, in July 1930. Hever started a bus service between Eynsford and Dartford. East Surrey competed on this route using a small Guy saloon. However, this did not affect Hever's operation too much, and the service was diverted to serve Farningham and Sutton-at-Hone. Hever took stock of four front-entranced 20-seat Bean saloons during 1928. KP4275 carried Eaton bodywork; whilst YX7518 was bodied by Holbrook. The final pair were bodied by Willowbrook and carried registration marks KO8824 and KO9958. These four vehicles were numbered 23, 21, 22 and 24 by Hever, and retained these rolling stock numbers when acquired by East Surrey in July 1930. They continued operating with their new owner until September 1931, when they were withdrawn, never seeing service with London Transport.

Another competitor for East Surrey and Hever came from the Sevenoaks Motor Services. This concern originally used a 14-seat Chevrolet before purchasing a Holbrook bodied Bean registered GJ3390, which seated twenty. Arriving in July 1930, it was soon supported by a 14-seat Willowbrook bodied Bean registered GJ5077. Both vehicles passed to East Surrey in November 1930, with GJ3390 being sold to AutoCar of Tunbridge Wells; whilst GJ5077 passed to London General Country Services and later London Transport.

MV933 was one of three Birch bodied Bean 14-seat saloons to be purchased by Royal Highlander for use on route 211 between Greenford and Ealing Broadway. It took fleet number BN1 under London Transport ownership and is captured by the camera in Greenford. *D.W.K. Jones Archive/ S.J. Butler Collection*

Royal Highlander took advantage of the extension of the Underground in North London. They introduced route 211 between Ealing Broadway and Greenford (Hare & Hounds). The route featured a number of projecting trees. To allow for this, three narrow Birch bodied Bean 14-seaters were purchased by the company during 1931, registered MV933, HX3466 and HX3467. A second route was added in May 1932, this being the 225 between Greenford and Haven Green. London General acquired the business in September 1932. However, the vehicles were in a poor condition, with the 225 being suspended for a short while to allow the vehicles to be repaired. They later transferred to London Transport, becoming BN1 to BN3. BN2 lasted with its new owner until 1934, whilst BN1/3 operated with London Transport until July 1936.

The Pinner Bus commenced operation of a route in March 1930, linking the Red Lion, Pinner and the Pinner Hill Golf Club. This bought with it an 18-seat Bean saloon registered MY3496 which was acquired along with Pinner Bus in September 1930. It gained rolling stock number BN4 and was first withdrawn in January 1931. However, it was soon reinstated at Hounslow, where it continued operating until 1935.

H.F. Phillips of Hornchurch used an older Bean saloon registered DV5364 on a works service for Ford, operating between the factory and Dagenham Dock Underground Station. The route was taken over by London Transport in December 1933, the Bean taking up fleet number BN5. However, it was not operated by London Transport.

Henry Turner of Wandsworth was operating two Bean saloons, a 25cwt (YN4594) and 30cwt (UL1771) model, both featuring rear entrance bodywork constructed by Birch Bros. Wearing a green livery, they were used on route 207 between Barnes and Richmond. Turner ran into financial problems in 1930, with the buses being repossessed by Birch. Both vehicles subsequently passed to other operators.

London Transport Passenger Board purchased two 14-seat Bean saloons taken into stock from St Albans and District in November 1933. Registered UR6278 and UR6279, they were operated for a year before being withdrawn in November 1934.

The Slough area of Berkshire was home to a number of small operators. Two of these, F. Berry and F.C. Owens, operated a solitary Bean bus each. KX4018 was a 14-seater operated by Berry; whilst RX7554 was a larger 20-seater Bean saloon operated by F.C. Owens. Both vehicles were acquired by London Transport in March and February 1934 respectively. Both were used on service 441 connecting Windsor Castle with Farnham Royal. KX4018 was withdrawn by London Transport in September 1934, with RX7554 being withdrawn in October.

The Rainham, Grays, Tilbury and Purfleet areas of Essex were the same as Slough, with a number of small independent bus operators plying for hire. One operator of interest from this area was Stephen's Rainham Bus Service. They operated an 18-seat Strachan bodied Bean saloon registered EV2060. The vehicle was used on services in the Rainham area, as well as one connecting Rainham with Upminster. The two routes were acquired by London Transport in March 1934, the Bean saloon passing to London Transport at this time.

Small Dennis saloons

The Dennis 30cwt was used by two operators in the Romford area during the late 1920s, early 1930s. These were Romford & District and Imperial. Both operators were using the smaller Dennis 30cwt saloon on routes that entered housing estates in the Romford and Rainham areas. Romford & District was acquired by London Transport in July 1934. Four Dennis 30cwt saloons were operated at this time, registered VA4584, EV4010, GJ2307 and VX9897, these taking fleet numbers DM1 to DM4. DM1 carried bodywork by Strachan; DM2 was bodied by Metcalfe. DM3 and 4 were bodied by Duple, both sitting on the Dennis GL chassis. Imperial was acquired by London Transport in November 1934. The Dennis saloons were numbered DM5 to 8 by London Transport, these being registered VX3180, VX6739, VX7401 and VX7354. DM5 and DM7 both carried bodywork by Metcalfe; whilst DM6 and DM8 were both bodied by Thurgood. After overhaul, DM3-5/7 were allocated to Barking rather than Romford for use on the G5 in the Romford area. At this time, Romford garage was over capacity and could not accommodate these small buses. By the end of 1936, the DM-class had all been withdrawn and sold.

West Kent Motors was an operator running services on the edge of the London Passenger Transport Board area. Two routes had started in 1927, crossing into this area. One ran between Kemsing, Seal and Otford, these being operated by two Dennis 30cwt saloons, both of which carried bodywork by Vickers of Crayford. A second operated between Sevenoaks, Polhill, Halstead, Knockholt and Westerham Hill, with sections entering the London Transport area. The company was acquired by London Transport in October 1939, with three Dennis 30cwt saloons being purchased by London Transport. Registration marks KO6244, KO7272 and KR5018 were carried by the trio. Allocated to London Transport's Dunton Green garage, they remained operating with their new owners until January 1940, at which time they were withdrawn.

Gravesend & District Motor Services operated a number of local services in the Gravesend area of Kent. Three of these vehicles were Dennis 30cwt saloons, registered DY4622, KP59 and KP1587. These were acquired by London Transport in October 1933, along with five Dennis G saloons registered KP3796, 4951, 7159, KR438 and KR705. Withdrawal of these vehicles was spread between May 1935 and April 1936. Prior

DM7 (VX7401) was a Metcalfe bodied Dennis 30cwt saloon new to Imperial of Romford. It operated local routes in the Romford area until withdrawal in 1936. *D.W.K. Jones Archive/ S.J. Butler Collection*

VX7354 was another Dennis 30cwt new to Imperial of Romford. This vehicle carried bodywork by Thurgood and was numbered DM8 by London Transport. It is seen wearing the livery of its former owner. *D.W.K. Jones Archive/S.J. Butler Collection*

to withdrawal, some of these small buses were reallocated to Addlestone for use on services in the Weybridge area, or to Amersham.

Five Dennis saloons were acquired by London Transport in June 1934 from W. Eggleton Ltd of Woking. The company had operated a service between Woking and Addlestone. Three of these were Dennis 30cwt saloons registered PG3194, PG8716 and PH5276. The other two were Dennis GLs, these carrying registration marks PL5896 and PG7438. The first four vehicles remained with London Transport until April 1936, with PG7438 being sold immediately to Aldershot & District in June 1934.

London Transport took over the operation of Howe's Brown Bus, Englefield Green in March 1934. The acquisition brought with it a Dennis 30cwt registered GU7544 and a Dennis H registered XV6303. GU7544 was withdrawn by London Transport in November 1935, and XV6303 in April 1936.

Amersham & District were operating a solitary Dennis 30cwt (PP7700), a single Dennis G registered KX1326 and three Dennis GLs registered KX5923, KX5967 and KX8569. These all passed to London Transport in November 1933. PP7700 only lasted until 1934 when it was withdrawn. The others lasted until 1935, at which time they were withdrawn.

Edwards Motor Services operated a route between Rainham Station and Rainham Ferry using a Thurgood bodied Dennis GL saloon registered VX6341. London Transport took over the service in January 1934, the Dennis saloons operating with London Transport in April 1936.

The final operator in the London Transport area to be acquired was The Reliable Omnibus & Motor Coaches. Six Dennis saloons were operated on a route between Grays and Purfleet, with four being acquired by London Transport in May 1934.

GU7544 is another example of the Dennis 30cwt. This particular vehicle was new to Howe's Brown Bus of Englefield Green, the operations of this company being acquired by London Transport in March 1934. *D.W.K. Jones Archive/S.J. Butler Collection*

A pair of Dennis Gs were acquired registered VW6182 and VW7400. A solitary Dennis 30cwt registered GC1313 was also acquired. The final bus was a Dennis GL registered GP5047. The Dennis Gs and 30cwt were withdrawn in 1934; whilst the Dennis GL lasted until May 1936.

Dennis Dart

The Dennis Dart saloon had been purchased by London General in 1930 to replace older buses in the fleet, as well as to operate routes into new areas previously unserved. The Darts were used in the Central area and wore a livery of red with white window surrounds and black mudguards, complete with a silver roof.

The first of these, DA1 to DA20, began to arrive with London General in April 1930. DA1 (GF494) was allocated to Hounslow at this time, transferring to Uxbridge in June. DA2 and DA3 (GF493/2) also arrived in April, going straight to Uxbridge. DA4/5 were next to arrive in May, registered GF491 and GF7207, again being allocated to Uxbridge. DA6 (GF7216) was the last of the batch to be allocated to Uxbridge, arriving in June. They were put to use on routes 505 (Uxbridge–Richings Park) and 506 (Uxbridge–Cowley–Wraysbury–Staines). By November, DA15 (GK3075) had arrived at Uxbridge for new route 507 (Uxbridge–George Green–Slough–Windsor), the latter being stocked with the type once enough had arrived. Harrow Weald took stock of the next trio, these continuing the numbering system as DA7 to DA9 (GH8078-80), displacing S-type singles from routes 353 and 210A. These were joined by DA11/2 (GH8082, GK3049) in October and DA13 (GK3050) in November. Mortlake took stock of DA10 (GH8081) in October. The final members of the initial twenty Dennis Darts were allocated to Kingston. These took up rolling stock numbers DA14, 16, 17 and 20 (GK3070, 3090, 3100, 3132).

Further Darts arrived with London General in 1931, numbered DA21 to DA32. The first, DA21 (GK5342), was initially used as a works float vehicle at Chiswick works, allowing bodies to be swapped during overhaul. The others replaced older Dennis Darts which were due to undergo an overhaul. DA22 (GK5441), DA24/5 (GN2145/6) went to Harrow Weald. Uxbridge took stock of DA23 (GK5442), DA27 (GN4739), DA29 (GN4741) and DA32 (GO661). Hounslow gained DA26 (GN4738) and DA28 (GN4740). Mortlake took DA30 (GN4742) into stock, whilst Kingston was allocated the other member of this batch, DA31 (GO618).

The next eight, DA33-40 (GX5325/6/31/27/32/3, JJ4333/4), arrived between December 1932 and February 1933. All but DA40 were allocated to Hounslow, with DA40 being allocated to Hornchurch. The introduction of these new Darts at Hounslow allowed similar older vehicles to transfer to Kingston for use on route 198 and Harrow Weald where they were put to use on the 230.

DA41 and DA42 (JJ4373/4) were the last new Dennis Darts to be delivered to London General, arriving in May 1933. They were allocated to Hanwell garage for use on route 211.

Three Metcalfe bodied Dennis Darts were acquired by London Transport from Romford & District in 1934. These carried rolling stock numbers DA43 to DA45 (EV4011, 5909, ANO794). They were allocated to Barking upon takeover, being used on routes G5 (Romford–Noak Hill) and 252B in the Barking area. The trio moved to Enfield for use on route 205 (Chingford–Potters Bar–Cuffley) in 1937.

DA1-40 were sold by London Transport between January and March 1940, being replaced by the rear-engined CR-class saloons.

EV4011 was a Metcalfe bodied Dennis Dart new to Romford & District. London Transport allotted rolling stock number DA43 to this vehicle which was initially based in the Romford area. DA43 moved to Enfield in 1937 for use on the 205, and it is on this route that it is captured by the camera. *D.W.K. Jones Archive/S.J. Butler Collection*

Dennis Ace/Mace

London Transport had operated only four Dennis Ace/Mace saloons, all of which had been acquired from companies that were absorbed into the company during the 1930s. Gravesend and District was absorbed into London Transport in 1933 when the area around Gravesend had been split between London Transport and Maidstone & District. Prior to the takeover by London Transport, Gravesend and District had ordered two Dennis Aces, with London Transport taking this order on. The pair carried 20-seat Waveney bodywork, wearing a green and black livery, but neither entered service in the Gravesend area. DC2 (BPF493) was allocated to Guildford where it was used on the 448 between Peaslake and Guildford. DC1 (AKR937) was allocated to St Albans for use on services around that area. They were withdrawn from service in October 1937, by which time they had been reallocated to Crawley.

A solitary Dennis Mace saloon was purchased by High Wycombe based Penn Bus Company, registered BBH755. The company was purchased by London Transport in July 1935, at which time this saloon took up rolling stock number DC3. It remained in use at High Wycombe on route 455A until withdrawal in May 1939.

The final Dennis Ace to be acquired by London Transport arrived in October 1939 when they took over the operations of West Kent Motor Services. Registered CKL719, this Dennis Ace was not used by London Transport, being sold by them in January 1940.

DC1 (AKR937) was a more unusual Waveney bodied Dennis Ace saloon that had been ordered by Gravesend and District, with London Transport taking on the order as they had acquired the company before it arrived. However, it was allocated to St Albans not Gravesend. It is photographed in the yard of St Albans garage. *D.W.K. Jones Archive/S.J. Butler Collection*

Bedford WLB

London Transport inherited a total of twenty-five Bedford saloons from various independent operators that had operated in the country area. All but two of these saloons were given the class code BD. The majority of these vehicles were operated by London Transport in the Country area, with most being shared between St Albans, Dunton Green and Epping garages.

The operations and vehicles of Gravesend & District Bus Services were taken over by London Transport in October 1933. A single Duple bodied Bedford WLB was operated by this operator. Registered AKK458, this example took up rolling stock number BD4. Another Gravesend operator, Enterprise, was absorbed into London Transport in November. Three Bedford WLBs were operated at the time of takeover. AKM308, KJ4255 and KJ4256 were the vehicles concerned, these taking rolling stock numbers BD5, 18/9. London Transport acquired the business of Sunshine Saloon Coaches of Kingston in December. A pair of Bedford WLBs were operating with this company at the time London Transport acquired the business. Duple bodied WLB APC55 was new to the company in 1933 and was numbered BD10 by its new owner. A second Bedford WLB was operated, this time bodied by Wycombe. Registered PJ8430, it was new to G.F. Gorringe of Kingston, passing to G.H. Gillman of Kingston in February 1933. Two months later, the latter company was acquired by Sunshine Saloon Coaches. It was numbered BD23 by London Transport. In December 1933 it was used on private hire work, being reallocated to Brixton garage.

Three more Bedford WLBs were acquired in January 1934. Express Motor Services of St Albans; Victoria Omnibus Service of St Albans and T. Harwood of Weybridge were all acquired by London Transport during the month. Express Motor Services were operating a Duple bodied WLB of 1932 vintage. It was registered JH974 and numbered BD15 by London Transport. JH1300 was acquired along with the Victoria Omnibus Service operations. This followed on as BD16. T. Harwood's Bedford WLB was registered PJ1727, this becoming BD21 with London Transport.

Another five operators were taken over by London Transport in February 1934, these all bringing with them examples of the Bedford WLB. J.H. Burgess of Englefield Green was operating a WLB registered PJ1806. This was new to the Egham Motor Company in 1931, taken over by Burgess in November 1932. It was allocated fleet number BD22 with its new owner. Reliance Coaches of St Albans operated a solitary Bedford WLB registered JH2314. Thurgood bodywork was carried by this bus, which was numbered BD17 by London Transport. The Egham Motor Company operated a single Duple bodied WLB registered APB940. This took stock number BD9 when acquired by London Transport. West Thurrock based Harvey's Transport were operating two Duple bodied examples. These carried registration marks EV8977 and EV8978 and took up fleet numbers BD11 and BD12 with London Transport. The Albanian Bus Company was the last to be acquired in February. Again, this operator had a pair of Bedford WLBs, both carrying Strachan bodywork. These were numbered BD13 and BD14 by London Transport and carried registration marks JH550 and JH911. Alongside this, a Thurgood bodied Bedford WHB saloon registered JH2313 was operated, but did not gain a fleet number when acquired.

The operations of Purfleet Bus Services and Bluebell Services, Stanwell were acquired by London Transport in March. Each operator owned a solitary Bedford WLB saloon. AMY660 was bodied by Reall and was new to Purfleet Bus Services. It was numbered BD8 by London Transport. Bluebell Services operated a Duple bodied WLB

registered MB6324. This took stock number BD20. Both vehicles were new to their respective operators in 1932. Another two operators who used Bedford saloons were acquired by London Transport in April. Greenhithe & District Bus Services operated a pair of WLBs registered AGY485 and AKE725, the latter vehicle carrying Duple bodywork. These were numbered BD1 and BD3 by London Transport. The second operator was Berry of Slough. This operator was using a solitary Bedford WHG saloon registered KX7894, this not being numbered by London Transport. A Strachan bodied WLB was taken into stock from Reliable Bus Services of South Stifford in May. Carrying registration mark AHK434, this saloon was numbered BD2 when acquired by its new owner. Another two Bedford WLB saloons, both of which were bodied by Duple, were acquired in October 1934 from Warwick of Farnham Common. These were registered AMF595 and AMH881, these being numbered BD6 and BD7. The operations of Berkhamsted & District were acquired in January 1939. A pair of Thurgood bodied WLBs were operated by this operator. They were registered JH238 and JH5324, neither of which were numbered by London Transport.

In December 1935, BD2, 4, 6 and 11 were converted to ancillary vehicles, primarily being used as store vans. These were allocated to Northfleet (BD2), Windsor (BD4, 11) and Hertford (BD6). This latter vehicle was converted during the war to tow producer gas trailers.

The BD-class's demise came during 1938 and 1939 when they were withdrawn. All but the vans had left London by February 1940.

BD13 (JH550) was a Strachan bodied Bedford WLB new to the Albanian Bus Company. It is captured by the camera in Windsor. *D.W.K. Jones Archive/ S.J. Butler Collection*

AMY660 was new to Purfleet Bus Services. This was the only BD-class saloon to carry bodywork by Reall. It took rolling stock number BD8 with London Transport and is seen in St Albans. *D.W.K. Jones Archive/S.J. Butler Collection*

BD4 (AKK458) was one of four Bedford WLBs that were converted to vans by London Transport. New to Gravesend & District, it is photographed inside Windsor garage after conversion. *D.W.K. Jones Archive/S.J. Butler Collection*

LEYLAND CUB

The Leyland Cub was introduced in 1931. The first of this type was taken into stock in November 1933, originating with St Albans and District. This vehicle was registered JH2401, and although it was the first of the type to be taken into stock, it was allocated fleet number C76. This was due to it being a country area bus, and it did not receive a fleet number until 1935. Initially allocated to St Albans, it also saw service at a number of Country area garages. In April 1934 it moved to Northfleet, transferring to Slough later in the year. It remained operating in that area until withdrawal in 1938.

C76 proved popular with London Transport, leading to an order being placed for 1934 and 1935 delivery. The first was numbered C1 (AYB717), this single-decker being bodied by Chiswick. Allocated to Hounslow garage, it was put to use on the 237 (Hounslow Garage–Chertsey Station), working alongside similar sized Dennis Dart saloons. During its first few months of operation, it also saw service from Merton and Barking. From Merton it was used on the 225 between Raynes Park Station and Lower Morden. After moving to Barking, it was put to use on the 252, 252A and 252B. C1 had its petrol engine replaced by a diesel engine in June 1935 and in November it moved to the Country area. Allocated to Langley Road, Slough, it was swapped for C51. It remained in service with London Transport until being withdrawn in November 1940.

A further seventy-four Leyland Cubs were ordered by London Transport, entering service in the Country area. These took fleet numbers C2 to C75 (BXD631/27-9/32/0/3-700) and all were bodied by Short Bros. Unlike C1, these were all fitted with diesel engines from new. C2 to C8 arrived in March 1935 (C2-5) and April (C6-8), these being allocated to Northfleet for services in North Kent.

Dunton Green took stock of C9-11 for use on services in the Sevenoaks, Knockholt and Orpington areas.

C12 found itself allocated to Epping. Northfleet also took stock of six Leyland Cubs, these being numbered C13, 51, 65/7-9. St Albans were allocated eleven C-class saloons (C14, 28-31/3/5-9). Neighbouring garage Hertford took stock of C15-24, 70-2. C25-7 and C66 took up residence at Staines garage. C32 was a solitary example that was allocated to Chelsham. C34 and C40-4 were all added to Guildford's allocation. Leatherhead took stock of C45, this being used on services in the Surrey Hills area. C48-50/3/4, 62-4 were all allocated to Addlestone. C52/5-61 were added to Windsor's allocation for use on a service between Windsor and Slough. The missing four C-class Cubs were allocated to Amersham (C74/5) and Dorking (C46/7).

The Central area received their own Leyland Cubs, these being bodied by Weymann. Totalling twenty-two, they were numbered C77-98 (CLE105-26). C77-80/2 were delivered in March 1936, with C81/3-98 arriving in April. These

C18 (BXD643) shows off the smart bodywork built by Short Bros. Seventy-four Leyland Cubs were delivered to London Transport for Country area operation during 1935. *S.J. Butler Collection*

C23 (BXD648) is another fine example of the Leyland Cub. It is seen operating route 315 to Wheathampstead. *S.J. Butler Collection*

were purchased to replace other small buses that were operating with Central area garages. C80 and C82 were allocated to Mortlake for route 207 (Barnes Railway Hotel–Richmond Park). Hanwell received C77, 86/9 and C90 for use on route 211 between Greenford and Ealing Broadway. Enfield took stock of C78/9, 81/8, 94/6/7/8, these vehicles taking up service on the 205 (Cuffley–Chingford). Barking took stock of a small number of the type for the 252/A/B group of services. Those allocated to this garage were numbered C83 to C85. Harrow Weald took the remaining examples (C87, 91-3/5), and put them to use on the 221 between the Red Lion in Pinner and North Harrow Station.

For completeness, the final eight Leyland Cubs were used on a service branded 'interstation', providing a link between the main Central London railway stations. Numbered C106 to C113, these took up registration marks CLX543-550. These were built as a deck and a half, with bodywork being constructed by Park Royal. They wore a distinctive blue and cream livery. All eight were allocated to Old Kent Road where they remained for their careers with London Transport. Other than a slight disruption during the war, the Interstation service was operated until November 1950, at which time the route was taken over by RTs.

These small buses suffered from capacity issues during the war, giving way to larger buses. The Cub was used to replace the Dennis Dart saloons being used on Central Area services. By the start of the Second World War a number of routes were being operated by Leyland Cubs. In addition to those mentioned above, the 216 (Kingston–Staines, Bridge Street); 223 (West Drayton Station–Ruislip Station) and 224 (Stanwell–Staines, Bridge Street). However, as demand grew during the war,

C61 (BXD686) was one of seven C-class Leyland Cubs to be allocated to Windsor garage. It is seen keeping company with another Leyland Cub. *S.J. Butler Collection*

C90 (CLE118) represents the smaller batch of Leyland Cub saloons delivered to London Transport for use on Central area services. C90 was originally allocated to Hanwell garage for use on the 211. *S.J. Butler Collection*

the Cub was replaced by larger buses. Two new routes were introduced in 1940, the 238 between Emerson Park and Noak Hill; and a second, the 225 (Northwood Hills–Eastcote) in 1944, with both routes being operated by the C-class Cubs.

As mentioned above, C51 was swapped with C1, the former vehicle being allocated to the Central area garage at Barking. It remained a Central area vehicle until 1944, being withdrawn during the year.

Twenty-one C-class buses were sold for further use in Belgium after the war. A number of Central area Cubs were transferred to the Country area for use on new small bus services that had been introduced between 1948 and 1950. The Country area C-class saloons continued operating during the 1950s, eventually being replaced by the GS-class.

FORD TRANSIT

The Ford Transit was introduced in 1965 as a light commercial vehicle. Although primarily built as a van, the Transit was 'and is also' built as a minibus. The majority were built as integral vehicles and looked very similar to the van. The 1970s and 1980s saw a number built with more purpose-built bus bodies. Strachen, Dormobile and Carlyle all built bus bodies for the Transit chassis. It is these three body builders that became popular over the two decades mentioned, with the Ford Transit coming into its own post-deregulation, with many fleets purchasing the type for low-cost operation.

London Transport

The first Ford Transit, a demonstration model, was trialled in the Highgate area during 1972. Registered JUD103L, this vehicle was bodied by Strachens and was used in service on the C11 (Archway Station–Cricklewood Broadway). Following the success of this trial, a fleet of twenty similar Ford Transits were ordered by London Transport. They were based on the Ford Transit van chassis. Bodied by Strachens, they carried dual-purpose seats. Delivery of these twenty vehicles took a year to complete. FS1 and FS2 (MLK701/2L) were first to arrive in August 1972. FS3-8 (MLK703-8L) followed in September, with FS9-16 (MLK709-16L) arriving in October. It wasn't until March 1973 that the next members of the batch arrived. It was at this time that FS17 (MLK717L) put in an appearance, with FS18 (MLK718L) following in June. The batch was complete in August when FS19 and FS20 (MLK719/20L) arrived with London Transport. FS1-4 were allocated to Enfield for use on the W9 (Enfield Town–Southgate). FS5 to FS8 and FS19 were allocated to Stockwell for use on route P4 (Brixton–Brockley Rise). Bromley took stock of FS9-11 and put them to use on the B1 (Bromley Market Place and Etlham Church). The final members of the batch, FS12-8/20, were allocated to Highgate. From there they operated route C11. The Ford Transits lasted a few years on these services before being replaced by larger Bristol LH saloons. After this, the majority were sold.

FS18-20 were put to further use in October 1974 when a new dial-a-ride scheme was introduced between Golders Green station and Hampstead Garden Suburb, becoming the H2. They were reallocated to Finchley garage. This new initiative was successful, and an additional bus was ordered. FS21 (GHM721M) was bodied by Dormobile. It arrived in March 1975 and was allocated to Enfield. A demonstrator registered SCG385M was placed on loan from Dormobile in October 1974, returning to them in April 1975.

FS11 (MLK711L) represents the small batch of Stachen bodied Ford Transit minibuses taken into stock by London Transport in 1973. It was one of three allocated to Bromley for use on the B1. *Ian Armstrong Collection*

A new local service was introduced in Potters Bar in March 1977 numbered the PB1. This connected Potters Bar rail station with Oakmere Station and Rushfield. FS7/9, 17 (MLK707/9/17L) were transferred to Potters Bar for use on this service.

These were replaced on the PB1 in 1979 when FS21 transferred to Potters Bar for use on the route. It was joined in October and November by two new Dormobile bodied Ford Transits registered CYT22/3V. They took up rolling stock numbers FS22 and FS23 respectively. FS24-6 (CYT24-6V), allocated to Finchley, also arrived in November, replacing the older Transits on the H2. 1983 saw those operating the PB1 replaced by a pair of Dodge minibuses.

A third batch of Ford Transits were purchased in 1985 for use on the H2 service. These continued on from the previous vehicles, taking fleet numbers FS27 to FS29. These carried Carlyle bodywork and featured standard bus seats rather than dual-purpose seats like their predecessors.

With the exception of FS29, these Ford Transits had left London by 1992. In November 1989, FS29 transferred to Westlink, where it was put to use on route 602 between Feltham and Shepperton. Westlink was privatised in January 1994, with this vehicle transferring to the new owner. The Westlink operation was acquired by London United in September 1995, with FS29 passing to this new owner. It lasted another couple of years before being sold for preservation.

FS21 (GHM721N) was a Dormobile bodied Ford Transit allocated to Finchley garage for use on route H2 in the Hampstead Garden Suburb area of north London. It is photographed on layover at Golders Green bus station. *Ian Armstrong Collection*

FS29 was the last Ford Transit to be purchased by London Transport. Registered C501HOE, it was bodied by Carlyle. It is photographed at Golders Green bus station. *Ian Armstrong Collection*

Eastern National

The Eastern National Omnibus Company Limited won the contract for LRT service 193 (Romford–Hornchurch), taking up service on the route from 13 July 1985. Double-deckers were used by the company on the route for just over a year before changes were made. The section of route between Hacton Lane and Hornchurch was withdrawn, with the 193 being diverted to serve the Country Park Estate, this all taking place from 2 August 1986. It was from this date that the route was converted to minibus operation, with the Hornchurch Hoppa fleet name being used from this time. Five Carlyle bodied Ford Transit minibuses were put to use on the route from this date. Rolling stock numbers 0600 to 0604 were allocated to these buses which were registered C600-4NPU. These were taken into stock by Eastern National in July 1985. These were replaced by larger Mercedes-Benz minibuses in 1988.

Five Ford Transit minibuses were operated by Eastern National on route 193 in 1985. 600 (C600NPU) is seen at the Country Park Estate end of the route, heading towards Romford Market. *Mike Harris*

BRISTOL LHS/LH

The Bristol LH was a lightweight chassis constructed by Bristol Motors and offered a smaller single-deck model, the larger single-deck being the Bristol RE. The standard-length LH measured 9.1m, with other models being offered at the same time. One of these was the shorter 7.9m long version, the LHS. Both the LH and LHS were operated by London Transport.

London Transport

The success of the Ford Transits meant that they soon became too small for the routes that they were operating. One of these routes, the C11, was in need of larger vehicles. For this a handful of different types were inspected by London Transport to determine a suitable replacement. One of these vehicles was a Marshall bodied Bristol LHS6L 33-seat saloon registered VOD93K, this coming on loan from Devon General. London Transport chose the Bristol LHS chassis but decided to go with the Eastern Coach Works (ECW) 26-seat body.

The new type was classified 'BS' by London Transport, with the first six (BS1-6– GHV501-6N) entering service in August 1975. They replaced Ford Transits on the C11. Eleven further BS-class saloons arrived with London Transport over the autumn of 1976. BS7 and BS8 (OJD7/8R) were first to arrive in September, followed by BS9 (OJD9R) in October. Delivery was complete when BS10-7 (OJD10-7R) were taken into stock during November. These were used to replace the other Ford Transits on the B1, P4 and W9.

The type was short-lived in London, being replaced on these routes by the slightly larger BL-class Bristol LH saloon. The final members left London by July 1981, after route W9 was converted to BLs. They were all sold off for further use, some of them seeing service in the Channel Islands.

London Transport searched for a replacement for some of the remaining RFs in the fleet in the 1970s. One of the models placed under consideration was the Bristol LH. London Transport took an ECW bodied example on loan from Hants and Dorset, this leading to ninety-five of the type being purchased by the company. Becoming the BL-class with London Transport, these single-deckers were narrower than other single-decks in the fleet, measuring 7ft 6in.

The first eighty-two of the type entered the London Transport fleet in 1976. The first fifty-three of these took up rolling stock numbers BL1 to BL53 (KJD401-440P, OJD41-53R). BL1 and BL2 were first to arrive, doing so in February, BL3, 4, 6-14, 16/7 all following in March. These were initially sent to Aldenham before being allocated to garages. BL2 and BL6 moved to North Street, Romford for use as type trainers, BL8

BS17 (OJD17R) was the last of the shorter Bristol LHS saloons to be purchased by London Transport. This particular vehicle was taken into stock to replace Ford Transit minibuses on the P4. *Ian Armstrong Collection*

moving over to Chiswick at this time. In April, BL5, 15/8/9 and 21-8, with BL3/4/7/9, 11-5/7 were allocated to North Street at the same time, whilst BL5, 16/8 and 20 were allocated to Riverside garage in Hammersmith. Sutton took stock of BL6 for use as a type trainer. Two more arrived in May, these being BL29 and BL30. BL2 was allocated to Fulwell, with BL4 joining it, transferring from North Street. BL6 was allocated to Camberwell and BL15 moved from North Street to Riverside. BL31 to BL40 arrived with London Transport in June and BL1 moved from Aldenham to Sutton along with BL10/9, 21-9, 31. In July, BL6 moved from Camberwell to Sutton. BL30/2-6 were allocated to Fulwell. BL37 also moved to Fulwell, for use as driver training, although it soon moved on to North Street. Those allocated to North Street, Romford were put to use on the 247 (Brentwood–Romford, North Street) and 250 (Epping, St Margaret's Hospital–Romford Station). Those allocated to Riverside were used on the 290 between Richmond and Hammersmith.

In July BL41 to BL44 and BL47 were delivered. The gaps were filled in August when BL45/6/8/9 arrived. BL38/9, 41-4 were moved from Aldenham to Fulwell. BL50-3 completed the batch in September. BL40/5-51 found homes at Kingston, being stored at Fulwell prior to this. They were joined at Kingston by BL4/6/8, 17 and 40. The allocation of the type to Fulwell saw them put to use on routes 264 (Kingston–Sunbury–Hersham) in July, and route 206 (Hampton Court–Claygate) in August, with appearances on the 201 (Kingston–Hampton Court). Kingston's allocation operated on route 216 (Kingston–Staines) as well as on the 71 between Kingston and Leatherhead on Sundays. Sutton's allocation could be found operating between

Morden Station and Lower Kingswood/Walton-on-the-Hill on services 80 and 80A. However, allocation of the type at Sutton was short-lived, with several being transferred to Norbiton in October, these being BL26-8 and 31. They were put to use on the 215 (Kingston–Church Cobham) from the latter garage.

BL54 to BL58 (OJD54-8R) were taken into stock by London Transport during October and BL52 and BL53 were allocated to Kingston and Fulwell. More followed in November, taking up rolling stock numbers BL59 to BL67 and BL69, these carrying registration marks OJD59-67/9R. BL29 transferred from Sutton to Fulwell in November. BL53 transferred the short distance between Fulwell and Kingston during the month and BL54 to BL57 joined the fleet at Norbiton. The transfer of these BL-class saloons allowed route 201 to gain a full allocation of the type. The final BL-class saloons to arrive in 1976 did so in December numbered BL68, 70-81 and BL84 (OJD68R etc). BL8 and BL58 were both allocated to Kingston during December, whilst BL59 was used at Croydon as a type trainer.

1977 started with the arrival of five additional BL-class saloons. BL82/3/5-7 (OJD82/3/5-7R) all arrived in January. Route 250 was merged with route 247 in January 1977, this allowing BL37 to transfer from North Street to Kingston. Another released from this was put to use on the 247B between Romford Station and Ongar. BL58 made the move from Kingston to Croydon. The latter garage was also allocated BL60-4 in January which allowed the 234A (Purley–Hackbridge) to be converted from

New to London Transport in March 1976, BL12 (KJD412P) entered service from North Street, Romford on routes 247 and 250. It is seen heading to Romford Station on the latter service. *Ian Armstrong Collection*

BL29 (KJD429P) was originally allocated to Sutton for use on the 80 and 80A in June 1976. In the November of the same year, it moved to Fulwell for use on the 264. *Ian Armstrong Collection*

RF operation. Edgware received their first examples of the type in January, these being BL65-77 which were used on the 251 between Stanmore Station and Arnos Grove Station.

BL88-92 (OJD88-92R) followed in February. Norbiton received BL78 in February; whilst Kingston was allocated BL80 and Sutton took stock of BL81 and BL84 during the same month. The final allocations to be made in February were BL82 to Edgware and BL83 to Fulwell.

Hounslow received its first two BL-class saloons in March, these being BL79 and BL86. BL79 was used as a type trainer at Hounslow. BL87-9/91 were sent to Chiswick during March. Two further BLs were delivered to London Transport in April. These followed on from the January deliveries, becoming BL93 and BL94 (OJD93/4R). Hounslow received further examples of the BL-class in April when BL85-92 were allocated to the garage. Those allocated to Hounslow were used to convert routes 202 (Hounslow–Richmond) and 237 (Hounslow–Chertsey). The numbers needed for a full allocation on both routes was made up by the transfer of several other BLs into Hounslow. At this time, BL36 and 83 made the move from Fulwell; Norbiton sent BL78. BL80 moved from Kingston; BL81 and BL84 from Sutton; BL82 from Edgware and BL83 from Fulwell. The final BL arrived in May numbered BL95 (OJD95R). Several months passed before the last three BLs entered service. BL93-5 were allocated to Uxbridge in September. They were put to use on the 128 between Ruislip Station, Mount Vernon Hospital and Harefield Hospital.

January 1978 was not a good month for the BL-class routes operated in the Surrey area, with a number of these being cut. Hounslow's route 237 was altered at the end of

January, the section of route between Sunbury and Chertsey being withdrawn. From this date, the route operated between Sunbury, Hounslow and the new extension to Shepherds Bush Green. At the same time, it was converted to Routemaster operation. This led BL78-81/4 to transfer to Gillingham Street, Victoria, BL82 and BL83 to North Street, Romford and BL85 to Holloway. BL86 also left Hounslow at this time, moving to Chiswick works.

In January the 264 was withdrawn and there were frequency reductions on routes 201 and 216, the latter changes making five BL-class saloons redundant. January saw the transfer of BL4 from Kingston to North Street and BL26/7 from Norbiton to Kingston, the latter movements being a result of route 215 transferring between the two garages. The allocation of BLs at Fulwell moved on to the 270 (Richmond Station–Fulwell Garage), displacing a fleet of SMD-class saloons from the route. However, this was a short-term allocation, with DMS-class double-deckers replacing the BLs on the 270 in April.

Bromley gained a small fleet of BLs in April for use on the B1 (Eltham Church–Bromley North Station), displacing the fleet of BS-class Bristol saloons. At the same time, Bromley's route 146 (Bromley North–Downe) lost its fleet of RTs in favour of BLs. For the routes, BL3 was used as a type trainer, being joined by BL26/7/9, 30/2/3/4 which transferred from Fulwell. In June, BL80 joined these saloons at Bromley, transferring from Sutton.

Further cuts to services in Surrey were made in October. At this time the 206 was withdrawn, with route 215 being diverted to serve Hampton Court. Route 211 (Tolworth–Walton-on-Thames) was also converted to the BL-class, the type having been favoured over Leyland Swifts during the year. Operation of the 202 (Richmond–Hounslow) transferred from Hounslow to Kingston, leading to the transfer of BL86-9, 91 between the two garages. BL28 made the move between Norbiton and Kingston. BL90 transferred from Hounslow to Riverside; and BL92 moved to Uxbridge at this time.

A repaint programme commenced in 1979, with the BLs being repainted into an all-red livery. The allocation of BLs on the 71 were replaced once this service was withdrawn and replaced with the 265. Kingston gained Norbiton's allocation of BLs during 1979 when route 201 transferred across.

BL22 was the first of the type to undergo overhaul at Aldenham, this taking place during 1980. After this, many others of the type underwent the same treatment between 1981 and 1985, gaining an all-red livery upon repaint.

North Street, Romford's allocation of BLs on the 247 and 247B were replaced by longer Leyland National saloons in January 1980. Routes 201 and 265 were also withdrawn, with BLs from the latter route being re-allocated to the 71 on Sundays. Stockwell-based route P4 (Brixton–Brockley Rise) had its allocation of BS-class saloons replaced in August 1980. BL9, 10, 71/4, and 84/7 were all transferred to Stockwell at this time for use on the route. BL29 reached the end of its life in November when it suffered severe fire damage whilst operating the B1.

The remaining BS-class routes were converted to BL-class during 1981. Sutton lost its allocation of BLs in April, these being re-distributed to Croydon for route 234A, operating at this time between Purley and Streatham Garage. Withdrawals and sales of the class began during the year. BL1, allocated to Croydon, was given red livery relieved by a cream band below the windows, its look being completed by the addition of small gold fleet names.

1982 was not a good year for the BL-class. Route 202 was converted to MCW Metrobus operation; Croydon converted the 234A to Leyland Nationals. This type was also used to convert Bromley-based route 146. Hammersmith lost route 290, this moving to Fulwell, the BLs being replaced by MCW Metrobuses. Routes 215 and 216 at Kingston were also converted to Leyland Nationals. After this, the BLs were left operating route 128 from Uxbridge and route 251 from Edgware. They could also be found on routes B1 at Bromley, C1 operated by Holloway, the P4 from Stockwell and Enfield's W9.

In 1983 there were more blows for the type. The P4 was extended to terminate in Lewisham, using Leyland National 2 saloons displaced from Red Arrow work. Route 128 was allocated an additional vehicle, so BL58 transferred to Uxbridge. The C11 also needed an extra BL when it was extended to Brent Cross. The W9 was lost to Eastern National in 1985, seeing the BLs withdrawn from this route. A fleet of Leyland Nationals entered service on the B1 in November of the same year.

Of the original ninety-five BLs, just thirty-eight remained in service by the beginning of 1986, these operating routes 128, 251 and C11. However, the lack of capacity on the type meant that Metrobuses were put in service at peak times, the BLs being put to use on the 210.

BL36 and BL81 were put to use by London Transport on contract work in 1986 and 1987, these being allocated to the Selkent division. Those allocated to Holloway and Edgware were repainted red with a black skirt, relieved by a white band. The use of the BLs on the 128 from Uxbridge ceased in July 1988 when the route gained an allocation of LS-class Leyland Nationals.

Westlink put BL81 to use on routes 592 (Kingston–Stanwell) and 602 (Feltham–Shepperton) from their Hounslow Heath garage in July 1989. BL81 remained operating with Westlink until June 1991.

In July 1989 it was the turn of the C11 to be converted to new rolling stock. At this time, the route was lost to R&I who purchased new Dennis Dart saloons for the route. During November, the 251 was the final route to lose the type. After this time, some of the type were put to new use as driver training vehicles.

A brief re-appearance of BL85 in service took place between November 1993 and May 1994. It was used in the Orpington area with Roundabout fleet names,

BL84 (OJD84R) was allocated to Holloway garage for use on the C11. It is seen wearing the white waist band and black skirt livery. *Ian Armstrong Collection*

substituting for the MC-class whilst they underwent modifications. Once they returned, BL85 was put back to use as a driver trainer.

The London Buses operation was privatised in 1994. Fifteen BLs (BL1/2/4/28/34-6/49/57/65/9/78/81/85/91) passed to Centrewest for continued use as driver training vehicles. These were used by the new company until 1998, at which time they were withdrawn.

DODGE S56

A1 (NYN1Y) represents the pair of Dodge minibuses taken into stock by London Transport for Potters Bar local services. It is photographed inside Gillingham Street garage. *Jeff Lloyd*

D odge introduced the S50 group of models in 1979, these again being vans and light commercial vehicles. The type did not prove popular with London Transport.

A pair of Dodge S56 minibuses, complete with Rootes bodywork, were purchased by London Transport in 1982, both arriving in January 1983. Numbered A1 and A2, these vehicles were registered NYN1/2Y. They wore an all-red livery, complete with yellow doors. They were purchased for Potters Bar local service PB1, displacing Ford Transits. They entered service on the route in March and continued until June 1986 when the PB1 was lost to North Mymms Coaches. It was at this time that they moved south to Catford where they were used as driver training vehicles. In November 1988, they went on loan to Greater Manchester Buses, returning to London the same month. A2 was the first to be sold, leaving the London Buses fleet in June 1989. A1 continued to be used at Westbourne Park as a driver training vehicle until it was withdrawn in 1995.

MERCEDES-BENZ L608D

T he Mercedes-Benz L608D was first introduced in 1969, with production of the model ceasing in 1986. Two small batches of the type were used on London Regional Transport (LRT) services during the 1980s.

Eastern National Citybus

Eastern National was one of the first operators to win LRT contracts, taking on routes 193 (Hornchurch–Romford) and W9 (Enfield–Muswell Hill Broadway). Bristol VRTs were initially used on the 193 whilst the W9 was operated by the Bedford YMQ. In August 1986, the 193 was converted to minibus operation initially using a fleet of Ford Transits before being converted to the Mercedes-Benz L608D minibuses. Members of the batch were numbered 0201 (C201HJN), and 0225-44 (D225-44PPU). They were

226 (D226PPU) represents the small batch of Mercedes-Benz 608Ds taken into stock by Eastern National for route 462. Allocated to Hornchurch, these passed to Thamesway in July 1990. *Ian Armstrong Collection*

allocated to Hornchurch garage from July 1985. 0201/225-34 carried Reeve Burgess bodywork, whilst 0235-0244 carried Dormobile bodywork. In July 1989, 0201 gained an all-over advertisement for Allens of Romford. 0230-4 later moved to Ponders End where they were used on the 462.

Swiss Cottage station finds London Country (North West) Mercedes-Benz L608D MBM9 (C309SPL). The fleet used by the company on the 268 were branded Hampstead Hoppa as seen above. *Mike Harris*

London Country North West

London Country (North West) Limited won the contract for the 268 (Golders Green– Finchley Road) from 31 May 1986. The route was operated from an outstation at the Scratchwood service station on the M1 before moving to another outstation at Muswell Hill in April 1987. The 268 was operated by eleven Reeve Burgess bodied Mercedes-Benz L608Ds inherited from London Country Bus Services Limited in September 1986. These were numbered MBM1-4/6-12 (C301SPL etc). A livery of yellow and green with red and white stripes was worn by the batch, which gained Hampstead Hoppa fleet names. The route was lost to R&I Tours upon re-tender.

MERCEDES-BENZ 609D

The Mercedes-Benz 609D was one of the many second-generation minibuses introduced by Mercedes-Benz from 1986. Like its predecessor the L608D, the model did not prove popular in London.

London Buslines was the only operator of the Mercedes-Benz 609D on an LRT service. The company gained the contract for the C4 between Putney Bridge Station and Chelsea Harbour, taking it over from 1 April 1989. Four Robin Hood bodied Mercedes-Benz 609Ds were put to use on the service. Registered E459, 460, 468, 470CGM they wore a yellow and brown livery. The service was known as the Fulham Hoppa.

LEYLAND CUB

Crystals of Dartford operated a pair of Leyland Cub single-deckers on route 146 between Bromley and Downe. C924DKR was the second of the two. *Ian Armstrong Collection*

Manufactured between 1979 and 1987, the Leyland Cub came in three lengths, 6.7m, 7.2m and 7.7m. The Cub saw a number of orders from local authorities for welfare buses. The majority carried either Wadham Stringer or Reeve Burgess bodies, with other bodywork also being offered. Just two were operated on an LRT service.

Crystals of Dartford could trace its origins back to a taxi-only operation in the Kent town of Sidcup in 1970, acquiring their first minibus in 1972. In August 1985, the company won the tender for route 146 (Bromley North–Downe). They operated a pair of Leyland Cubs bodied by HTI Maxeta. They worked the route alongside a Wadham Stringer bodied Ford R1115 purchased in 1987. The route was extended in 1988 with other vehicles being ordered for the route. The Leyland Cubs were registered C923/4DKR and could seat thirty-three passengers.

IVECO 49.10

The Iveco 49.10 was one of four models developed under the Iveco Dailybus name, first introduced in 1978. The 49.10 was based on the 5 tonne van chassis and featured various bodywork. A number of the type were operated by operators in the Greater London area.

London Buses Limited

A low-cost minibus unit was established in the Orpington area of south-east London in 1986 named 'Roundabout Buses'. Five Optare CityPacer bodied Volkswagen LT55 minibuses were operated on the services, alongside a fleet of twenty-four Robin Hood bodied Iveco 49.10 minibuses on six routes, these being as follows:

R1 (Bromley Common–Green Street Green–Orpington–St Pauls Cray–Sidcup)
R2 (Orpington Station–Green Street Green–Biggin Hill Valley)
R3 (Petts Wood Station–Orpington–Chelsfield–Green Street Green–Orpington)
R4 (St Pauls Cray–St Mary Cray–Orpington–Locks Bottom)
R5 (Orpington Station–Green Street Green–Orpington Station)
R6 (Orpington Station–Green Street Green–Orpington Station)

Stock numbers RH1-24 were allotted to the batch which gained registration marks C501-12DYM, D513/4FYL, C515-21DYM, D522-4FYL. However, not all twenty-four were needed on the Roundabout network. Therefore, RH14, 19, 20 and 22 were retained by London Buses at Aldenham works, from where they were initially used on staff shuttles. These four were loaned to Eastbourne Buses during October 1986, returning to London between December 1986 and April 1987. RH19 and RH22 were both sent to Camberwell upon their return to the capital where they received an all-blue livery for use on the Chelsea Harbour Hoppa service C3, this route operating from the Battersea minibus base, the route transferring to Victoria Basement in September 1987. RH14 was allocated to Orpington when it returned from Eastbourne. RH20 was shared between Camberwell and Battersea and was used as a driver trainer. In November 1987, it gained a similar blue and cream livery to that worn by Eastbourne Buses. It was allocated to the low-cost Bexleybus operation based at Bexleyheath garage. The Ivecos lacked the required capacity on the Roundabout network, leading to the loan of some MCW MetroRiders that had been working for Bexleybus. By 1988, RH10-8, 20/1/3/4 had been transferred to Bexleybus, with RH1-9 being retained at Orpington.

In December 1992 the Roundabout Buses operation was absorbed into the main Selkent operation. At this time, the fleet of Ivecos were repainted all-over red with Roundabout fleet names. However, the RH days were numbered after this, with the majority leaving London in 1993/1994. RH1 was retained and was used on the Orpington area routes until the Roundabout operation ceased in December 1995.

The Bexleybus operation was wound down in January 1991. The RHs transferred back to Orpington, before being sold via London Bus Sales at Fulwell.

Eight Reeve Burgess bodied Iveco 49.10 minibuses were taken into stock by London Buses in December 1990. Taking up rolling stock numbers FR1-8 (H701-8YUV), these vehicles were allocated to Hounslow where they operated route H20. They wore an all-white livery, complete with a green stripe. They were operated by London Buses on behalf of the London Borough of Hounslow.

RH1 (C501DYM) was the first of twenty-four Robin Hood bodied Iveco 49.10 minibuses to be operated by London Buses in the Orpington area. It is seen departing Orpington town centre bound for Chelsfield wearing the distinctive Roundabout livery. *Ian Armstrong Collection*

1988 saw thirteen RH-class minibuses transfer to the Bexleybus operation based at Bexleyheath. Whilst operating with this company, they gained new local numbers. RH11 (C511DYM) was given local number 65 and is seen in Bexleyheath town centre on route B15. *Ian Armstrong Collection*

RH19 (D519FYL) was one of two Iveco 49.10s to be used by London Buses on Chelsea route C3, gaining an all-blue livery complete with Chelsea Harbour branding. It is seen on layover wearing this livery. *Ian Armstrong Collection*

Route H20 gained a fleet of eight Reeve Burgess bodied Iveco 49.10 minibuses in December 1990, these wearing a white and green livery. FR7 (H707YUV) is photographed on layover at Hatton Cross bus station showing off this livery whilst off route on the H24. *Ian Armstrong Collection*

A third variant of the Iveco 49.10 arrived in the spring of 1993, these carrying bodywork constructed by Marshall of Cambridge. The last of the batch, FM10 (K530EFL), is seen on layover at Petts Wood Station carrying Roundabout branding. *Ian Armstrong Collection*

Ten Marshall bodied Iveco minibuses were added to the Selkent fleet in April and May 1993. Orpington took stock of FM1-10 (K521-30EFL) which replaced older RH-class Iveco minibuses on the Roundabout routes.

London Country (North West) Limited

Route 153 was another route to be converted from double-deck to minibus operation in the late 1980s. The section of route between Angel Islington and Tottenham Court Road Station was withdrawn from 4 April 1987. It was at this time that London Country (North West) took over operation of the route, converting it to a minibus route. A fleet of Robin Hood bodied Iveco 49.10 minibuses were used on the route from an outstation that the company established in the Muswell Hill area. The vehicles concerned were registered D21-6RPP and D472/3RVS. Rolling stock numbers MBI57/8, 64/3/5/2/1/0, 59 were allocated to these midibuses. Holloway Hoppa fleet names and route branding were carried by these buses. The 153 was lost to London Buses in June 1988.

London Country (North West) employed a fleet of Robin Hood bodied Iveco 49.10 minibuses on the 153. D473RVS represents the batch when photographed on Holloway Road. *Mike Harris*

R&I Tours

R&I Tours commenced operation of LRT services 268 (Golders Green–Finchley Road Station) and H2 (Golders Green–Hampstead Garden Suburb) in June 1989. They used a fleet of Robin Hood bodied Iveco 49.10 minibuses, these wearing a silver and blue livery. The batch was split in two featuring different seating capacities. F201-7HGN were 23-seaters and were put to use on the 268.

The final three carried nineteen seats and were used on the H2. Originally registered F208-10HGN, they were late in arriving and were re-registered G208-10LGK. They were joined by two additional minibuses, these carrying registration marks G211/2LGK. These were employed on the H17 (Harrow–Sudbury) after R&I took up the route.

F205HGN represents the small fleet of Iveco 49.10 midibuses operated by R&I Tours on route 268. Bodied by Robin Hood, it is photographed on layover at Golders Green bus station. *Ian Armstrong Collection*

G61JVV was one of four Robin Hood bodied Iveco 49.10 minibuses loaned to Stagecoach Selkent in 1994 from United Counties. They were repainted all-over red and used on the Bromley Christmas park & ride service. *Michael Wadman*

Stagecoach London

By the time privatisation came around in 1994, just three RH-class Iveco 49.10 minibuses were still in use on London services. RH1, 5 and 22 were still in use at Orpington when Stagecoach took over Selkent on 6 September 1994. These remained in the Stagecoach Selkent fleet until February 1996 when they were sold, with RH1 being sold for preservation.

At the same time, the Marshall bodied Iveco minibuses also transferred to the Stagecoach Selkent operation. FM1-10 continued to be used in the Orpington area until they left the capital in November 1995. They passed to Stagecoach Midland Red, operating in Rugby.

Just after acquisition by Stagecoach, four similar Iveco minibuses were loaned from fellow Stagecoach operator United Counties for use on the seasonal Bromley Park & Ride. F58-60AVV and G61JVV were numbered RH58-61 for the duration of their stay, gaining a repaint into all-red. Stickers were placed on the vehicles to advertise the service. Allocated to Bromley, they were retained until January 1995 when they returned to their rightful owner.

London United

London United was privatised on 5 November 1994. At this time, FR1-8 (H701-8YUV) transferred to their ownership. They continued to operate the H20 from Hounslow until early 1997, being sold in February.

VOLKSWAGEN LT55

The Optare CityPacer bodied Volkswagen LT55 was one of the first purpose-built minibuses of the 1980s. London Buses Limited took stock of their first CityPacers, which they allocated the OV class code, in July 1986. OV1-5 (C525DYM, C526-8DYT, D529FYL) were allocated to the low-cost Roundabout operation in Orpington. These 25-seaters worked alongside the Robin Hood bodied Iveco minibuses 'mentioned in the previous chapter on Roundabout services' in August. These remained in service until 1990 when they were replaced by similar,

The first five Optare Citypacer bodied Volkswagen LT55 minibuses taken into stock by London Buses were allocated to the Roundabout operation in Orpington. The last of the five, OV5 (D529FYL), is seen showing off the Roundabout livery whilst heading to Petts Wood Station on route R3. *Ian Armstrong Collection*

slightly newer vehicles from London General. After this, OV1-5 were used as driver training vehicles before finally being withdrawn from service in 1991 and 1992. In June 1991, OV2 (C526DYT) was donated to the London Transport Museum where it is displayed wearing the Roundabout livery.

The first of nineteen CityPacers arrived in September 1986. Numbered OV6 to OV24, they were registered D338-356JUM; the others followed in October. They were allocated to Victoria and put to use on new central London route C1 (Westminster–Victoria–Kensington). They also saw service on the C20 and C21 in the evening. The basement of Victoria garage became the new minibus base; becoming known as Victoria Basement, it was allocated its own garage code, this being VB. Even though this batch had been allotted rolling stock numbers, they were not applied until November 1988. Between their arrival and this date, the batch were referred to by their registration marks. The Volkswagen chassis did not fare well in London conditions, these being withdrawn by 1990. After this time, a handful were briefly used as driver trainers before being sold.

A further twenty-five Optare CityPacers were purchased by London Buses Limited between December 1986 and February 1987. They took up rolling stock numbers OV25 to OV49 (D357-81JUM). They were placed on loan with London Country (North West) Ltd upon arrival, the latter company taking on the contract for new route C2 between Regents Street and Camden Town in March 1987. They were numbered MBV27-51 by

Five additional Optare CityPacers were allocated to the Roundabout operation in 1989/1990. OV26 (C526DYT) was one of these and is again seen on its way to Petts Wood Station whilst operating the R3. *Ian Armstrong Collection*

London Country (North West) who opened a new midibus base in Muswell Hill. Some transferred to Garston after delivery for use as driver trainers. However, the C2 was not operated for long by London Country, passing to London Buses Limited in June 1988, at which time they took up their intended OV-class fleet numbers. They were added to the midibus allocation at Victoria Basement, joining OV6-24.

The end of 1989, beginning of 1990 saw a number of the OV-class transfer around London Buses. OV25, 26, 38, 44/9 transferred to the Roundabout operation in Orpington. OV43 and OV45 were reallocated to Walthamstow. At the same time, Westbourne Park took stock of OV27, 35/6/9, 46-8 and put them to use as driver training vehicles. They were also used at other garages as the need arose.

The final trio of CityPacers were taken into stock for use on a new service introduced to connect the main Central London rail termini. Numbered OV50-52 (E998, 99TWU and E638TWW) they were different from the others, being fitted with rear doors, allowing them to carry wheelchair passengers. The contract started in March 1988 and was branded 'Carelink'. Victoria Basement was again the garage chosen to house them. The contract was lost in October 1992 to F.E. Thorpe with OV50-2 transferring to Thorpes at this time.

A number of Optare CityPacers were loaned to London Buses Limited during 1989 from Yorkshire Rider, being used for driver training duties in west London. E211PWY was first to arrive in June, with E205PWY also being used during the same month.

OV35 (D367JUM) is seen operating the 153 to Archway Station wearing a basic red livery, relieved by prominent London General fleet names. *Ian Armstrong Collection*

The final three OV-class Optare CityPacers were used on a route linking the main London railway termini, these being branded as Carelink. OV50 (E998TWU) is captured by the camera outside King's Cross station. *Mike Harris*

The latter vehicle was used from Hanwell. E207PWY followed, being allocated to Acton Tram Depot, along with E211PWY. In August another two registered E206/14PWY arrived, these again being allocated to Centrewest's Acton Tram Depot. All of these returned to Yorkshire during August.

METRORIDER

This chapter takes a look at the MetroRiders, both MCW (Metro-Cammell Weymann) and Optare, that have operated in the capital. Over 200 of the type were purchased by operators for use on London services. Two lengths were operated, the shorter MR-class which measured 7.0m, and the longer MRL-class which measured 8.4m. The MetroRider was an integral bus, with features being taken from the Optare CityPacer. MCW got into trouble in 1989, the design of the MetroRider being sold to Optare, Leeds who continued producing the model with the same success as MCW.

London Buses Limited

One hundred and thirty-four MCW MetroRiders were purchased by London Buses Limited, arriving between 1987 and 1988. The first twenty-two arrived at Kingston in June 1987, operating with the Westlink operation. They were put to use on local area routes K1 (Surbiton Station–New Malden Police Station), K2 (Kingston Hospital–Kingston–Hook) and K3 (Kingston, Cromwell Road–Esher High Street). Rolling stock numbers MR1 to MR22 were allocated to the batch, these being registered D461-82PON. A livery of red with white and turquoise stripes was worn by these minibuses. An extra MetroRider was added to Kingston's allocation in January 1988. MR134 (D482NOX) was a former demonstrator.

MR23 to MR52 (E132-52KYW) were next to arrive. MR23-5 arrived in September 1987, followed by MR26-31 in October. MR32-53 completed delivery in November. All were allocated to the low-cost Harrow Buses operation, operating from a garage in North Wembley. Harrow Hoppa branding was applied to these vehicles, along with a red, cream and black livery.

The final deliveries of MRs in 1987 also arrived in November. They were ordered for the Bexleybus operation in the Bexleyheath area. However, before entering service with Bexleybus, MR53-64 (E929/30KYR, E631-40KYW) were placed on loan with Roundabout Buses in Orpington. They remained there until January 1988, at which time new MRL-class MetroRiders arrived at Orpington. MR53-64 moved to Bexleyheath at this time. They wore the distinctive blue and cream livery associated with Bexleybus and took local fleet numbers 29 to 40.

Streatham was in receipt of six shorter MetroRiders in July 1988. Originally numbered SG1 to SG6 (E873/4NJD, F895-8OYR), they gained fleet numbers MR93-8 in August. These saloons were put to use on the G1 (Clapham Junction–Tooting Broadway–Furzdown) and G2 (Wandsworth–Tooting Broadway–Furzdown), serving St George's Hospital in Tooting, being operated on behalf of the Wandsworth Hospital Authority, whose name was adorned on the sides of the vehicles.

Routes K1, K2 and K3 in the Kingston area were the first routes in London to gain a fleet of MetroRiders, with twenty-two being allocated to the Westlink operation. MR6 (D466PON) represents this batch and is seen heading to New Malden Station on the K1 wearing the red with white and blue stripes livery. *Ian Armstrong Collection*

MR33 (E133KYW) represents the thirty-strong batch of MetroRiders allocated to the Harrow Buses operation. It is seen on local route H11 passing Harrow bus station wearing the red, cream and black livery. *Ian Armstrong Collection*

The final twelve MCW MetroRiders to be delivered in 1987 were destined for the Bexleybus operation but were temporarily diverted to Roundabout Buses. They eventually moved to their intended garage in January 1988. MR56 (E632KYW) represents the batch and is photographed on layover in Bexleyheath town centre. *Ian Armstrong Collection*

MR57 (E633KYW) was given local fleet number 33 whilst operating with Bexleybus. The low-cost operation used a blue and cream livery as seen above. MR57 is photographed at Bexleyheath station. *Mike Harris*

The first of the longer MRL-class MetroRider put in an appearance in January 1988 with MRL65 to MRL76 (E641-50KYW, E705/6LYU) arriving in London at this time. These were allocated to the Roundabout Buses operation in Orpington, displacing MR53-64. MRL77 and MRL89-92 (F197YDA, F193-6YDA) were also allocated to Orpington, arriving in October 1988.

The gap was filled by MRL78-88 (F182-92YDA), these also being delivered during October. They were allocated to the Westlink operation centred on Kingston. These eleven minibuses replaced a similar number of shorter MR-class saloons. MR9-10 moved to North Wembley, MR11-3 to Sutton and MR14-22 to North Street, Romford.

Electronic retarders were fitted to the MetroRider fleet over the summer months of 1988. To cover for the vehicles having this work done, six short MetroRiders were taken on loan from Northumbria Motors Services between July and October. The vehicles concerned were registered E823-7/9BTN, the first four being allocated to North Wembley for the duration of their stay; whilst the last two were allocated to Westlink.

MRL70 (E646KYW) was one of the new, longer MCW MetroRiders taken into stock by the Roundabout operation, displacing the loaned Bexleybus MetroRiders. It is seen travelling through Orpington town centre on route R1. *Ian Armstrong Collection*

Eleven MRL-class MetroRiders were allocated to the Westlink operation in October 1988, displacing some of the first batch of MR-class saloons. MRL86 (F186YDA) is seen in Kingston on its way to Hook. *Ian Armstrong Collection*

October and November 1988 saw the final thirty-five MCW MetroRiders taken into stock by London Buses. These comprised seven short MRs (MR99-105) and twenty-eight longer MRLs (MRL106-133). Registration marks F99-133YVP were allotted to these vehicles. MR99-105 were allocated to Walthamstow for use on routes W11 (Walthamstow, Crooked Billet–Walthamstow Central Station), W12 (Wanstead–Walthamstow) and W15 (Hackney Central Station–Walthamstow Central Station). MRL106-112 joined them on these services. MRL113-133 were intended for Clapton but were loaned to Walthamstow from November 1988 until May 1989. Once at Clapton, these saloons took up service on the 100 between Wapping and Aldgate. The service was branded as Wapping Citylink and commenced operation in June 1989.

Harrow Buses were unsuccessful at retaining the midibus routes in that area in 1990, with Sovereign and Metroline taking the routes over. This led to the fleet of MetroRiders being reallocated around London Buses. Dennis Darts were introduced to the Roundabout operation during 1990, seeing the MetroRiders transfer to Bromley and Bexleyheath. The latter transfers allowed London Buses to serve more housing estates that had yet to gain a bus service. The Bexleybus operation ceased in January 1991,

with the majority of the MetroRiders being retained at Bexleyheath under the London Central name, the blue and cream livery being lost in favour of the traditional red livery.

An Optare MetroRider demonstrator registered G689KNW arrived in January 1990. It saw service at a handful of garages over the course of the year. These were Orpington, Clapton, Walthamstow, Westbourne Park and Potters Bar. It transferred to Kentish Bus in January 1991 for use on the B11 at Northfleet.

The first of a batch of Optare MetroRiders arrived in London during July 1990 numbered MRL135 (H135TGO). Upon arrival it was added to Sutton's allocation. Another twenty-four, MRL136-159 (H136-59UUA), arrived between December 1990 and January 1991. MRL136-40/55-9 were allocated to Bexleyheath, whilst MRL141-54 were added to Plumstead's allocation. Those at Bexleyheath were used on the B12 (Erith–Bexleyheath), B13 (Bexleyheath–Avery Hill Road) and B16 (Bexleyheath Garage–Eltham Station), whilst those at Plumstead were put to use on the 380 (Lewisham–Abbey Wood Station) and 386 (Eltham High Street–Greenwich Hospital). MRL142-5 were placed on loan with the Roundabout operation in Orpington in December 1990, returning to Plumstead in January 1991.

MRL126 (F126YVP) shows off the branding applied to a fleet of MetroRiders allocated to Clapton. The 100 was branded as the Wapping Citylink in 1989. *Ian Armstrong Collection*

MRL136 (H136UUA) was the first of twenty-four Optare MetroRiders to be allocated to Bexleyheath in the summer of 1990. It is seen in Bexleyheath operating the B16 to Kidbrooke. By the time these buses entered the fleet, the Bexleybus operation had ceased, and Bexleyheath garage was placed under the control of London Central. *Ian Armstrong Collection*

Selkent received the next consignment of Optare MetroRiders over the summer of 1991. MRL160-8 arrived in May, followed by MRL169-176 in June. These carried registration marks H160-176WWT. Allocated to Bromley, they displaced DT-class Dennis Darts which moved across to Fulwell.

London General took stock of thirty-three Optare MetroRiders between June and September 1991. Registered H677-90YGO, J690-9, 710, 701-9CGK, they took stock numbers MRL177 to MRL209. MRL177-80 were first to arrive, putting in an appearance in June, followed by MRL181-93 in July and MRL194-203 in August. MRL204-9 completed the delivery, arriving in September. All were initially allocated to Victoria Basement to replace the unreliable OV-class Optare CityPacers. They were given Streetline branding and used on route C1. MRL177-83 did not last long at Victoria Basement, moving to Sutton in August 1991 for use on the 413 (Belmont Station–Sutton Garage).

London Northern was the recipient of the next twenty-one MetroRiders. MRL210-6 arrived in November 1991, MRL217-9 in January 1992, with MRL220/1 completing the order in February. Allocated to Holloway for routes W4 and W5, they carried registration marks J210-21BWU.

The final MetroRider to be allocated to Victoria Basement arrived in February 1993, registered K223MGT (MRL223). This solitary vehicle joined others at Victoria on the C1. The closure of Victoria Basement in January 1994 meant that the MRLs were redistributed between a new minibus base in Battersea or Stockwell.

MRL224-41 (K424HWY etc) also arrived in February 1993, and were allocated to Bexleyheath. They were predominantly used on routes 278 (Kidbrooke–Lewisham) and 244 (Woolwich–Belmarsh Prison–Thamesmead). These featured a wider front destination display, along with two-piece doors.

A special one-off part of an Optare MetroRider was constructed for display at the London Transport Museum in Covent Garden. It took fleet number MRL242.

MRL166 (H166WWT) was one of seventeen Optare MetroRiders that were allocated to Selkent's Bromley garage to displace Dennis Dart saloons. It is seen on its way to New Addington on route 314. *Ian Armstrong Collection*

MRL193 (J693CGK) was part of a thirty-three strong fleet of Optare MetroRiders delivered to Victoria Basement garage as replacements for the Optare CityPacer minibuses. It is seen loading at Victoria on its way to Clapham Junction. *Ian Armstrong Collection*

London Northern were allocated twenty-one MetroRiders for routes W4 and W5, these being allocated to Holloway. MRL214 (J214BWU) represents the batch and shows off the route branding applied for the W4. *Ian Armstrong Collection*

Following the closure of Victoria Basement, MRL194 (J694CGK) was one of many Optare MetroRiders to transfer to the Battersea Bridge midibus base. It is seen on layover at Clapham Junction having completed a journey on the C3. *Ian Armstrong Collection*

London Central's Bexleyheath garage took stock of the final batch of MetroRiders to be purchased by London Buses, these being shared between routes 244 and 278. MRL229 (K429HWY) is photographed on route 278. *Ian Armstrong Collection*

Westlink/London United

Westlink was the first of the former London Buses Limited divisions to be privatised, this taking place in January 1994. At this time, MR1-7, 10/1, 23, 30/1/4/9, 42/7, 52, 134 and MRL78-92 were transferred to the new operator. Soon after privatisation, MRL78 to MRL80 were fitted with tail-lifts to allow wheelchair access to the vehicles. They were put to use on the H20, operating on behalf of the London Borough of Richmond. They gained private registration marks A2, 3, 4LBR. Westlink was sold to London United on 15 September 1995.

Cowie/Arriva London

The Cowie Group purchased Leaside Buses in September 1994, followed by South London in January 1995. Leaside was operating a trio of MCW MetroRiders (MR102/4/5), these being operated on a contract for the Department of Health and Social Security (DHSS) Clapton garage. South London were operating MCW MetroRiders MR29, MRL107, 122-4/7/9, 133 from Thornton Heath and MR46, 93-8 from Norwood.

MR93-6/8 were placed on loan with Stagecoach East London in April 1995 for use on the P14. They were returned a couple of months later in June.

The operations of Arriva Croydon and North Surrey were transferred to the control of Arriva London South on 30 October 1999. Five Optare MetroRiders were acquired

Cowie South London took stock of a small number of MetroRiders from London Buses when it took over the operations in January 1995. MRL124 (F124YVP) was one of those allocated to Norwood for route 249. It is seen passing through Crystal Palace on its way to Tooting Bec Station. Yellow stripes at the rear were applied to the Cowie London fleet. *Ian Armstrong Collection*

along with the Beddington Farm garage. They were numbered MRL440-3, 472 (M440-3HPF, P472APJ).

Arriva London was the last operator of the MR-class MetroRider. The trio used on the DHSS shuttles were replaced on the contract between Waterloo and Westminster by a similar number of Plaxton Pointer MPD bodied Dart SLFs.

London Central/Go Ahead London

London Central was privatised on 22 September 1994, being purchased by the Go-Ahead Group. From this date, MCW MetroRiders MR57, 99, 100, 103 were acquired, these being allocated to Peckham. Optare MetroRiders MRL136-40, 155-9, 224-41 were also operating with London Central at this time, these all being allocated to Bexleyheath. On 2 November, London General was purchased by its management, being acquired by the Go-Ahead Group in 1996. Optare MetroRiders MRL135, 177-209, 223 were operating from Sutton, Merton and Stockwell garages at this time.

Little happened with these vehicles for the duration of their stay with either operator. MRL135, 194-7 transferred from Stockwell to Merton when the C3 (Earls Court–Clapham Junction) transferred between them. MRLs were replaced by low-floor Plaxton Pointer bodied Dennis Dart SLFs in December 1996. At this time, they moved

Under the control of London General, a number of Optare MetroRiders passed to Merton garage for further use. MRL209 (J709CGK) is seen on its way to Wimbledon Station on route 156. London General continued the Streetline branding introduced by London Buses. *Ian Armstrong Collection*

to Battersea for route 239 (Victoria–Clapham Junction) and Putney for the 265 (Putney Bridge–Tolworth), replacing the MA-class at the latter garage. January 1998 saw MRL177, 194/7, 200/2/4/7/8, 223 transferred to Merton, replacing SR-class Optare StarRiders. MRL177 lost its cherished registration mark (VLT277) in favour of its original one, H677YGO, in February.

Metroline

At the time of privatisation, 7 October 1994, Metroline was operating one MCW MetroRider. MR20 was allocated to Edgware at this time. It remained with Metroline until January 1997; at which time it was sold to F.E. Thorpe.

Stagecoach London

The Stagecoach Group purchased East London and Selkent on 6 September 1994. Both the MCW and Optare MetroRiders were in use with both companies at this time. East London were operating MR16 from Stratford; this also being where longer MRL65-77, 106/9-14/8-21/5/6/8, 130-2 were operating from. Selkent were operating MR27 and 46 from Catford. Longer MRL141-54, 160-76 were shared between Plumstead and Bromley.

MRL109 (F109YVP) was one of many MetroRiders taken into stock by Stagecoach East London, these being allocated to Stratford. It is seen on layover at Stratford bus station complete with East London Hoppa fleet names. *Ian Armstrong Collection*

South London loaned MR93-6/8 to East London in April 1995 for use on the P14. They returned to their rightful owner in June. Stagecoach gained the contract for one of the East London line rail replacement services. MRL130 gained an orange and white livery for the route in April 1995. MRL144 was treated to a similar livery in early 1996.

May 1995 saw the arrival of an MCW MetroRider from Stagecoach Coastline Buses. 2901 (F561HPP) was allocated to Selkent's Plumstead garage to provide cover for an increase on route 380. It retained its Stagecoach stripes and was operated carrying Stagecoach South legal lettering. MR27 and MR46 were withdrawn in May, passing to Stagecoach Busways. Other members of the type were also withdrawn in 1995. MR46 returned to Selkent in September 1995, and carried fleet number 1645. It was operated from Orpington whilst wearing Stagecoach stripes. Others were hired from Busways in October 1995 to cover for three DT-class Darts that transferred from Orpington to Bromley for use on the seasonal park & ride service. Former Selkent MR27 (E127KYW), carrying fleet number 1644, was joined by 1692/3 (K165/6FYG) from Busways, Newcastle. They returned north in November along with MR46. In February 1997, MRL141 was transferred from Selkent to East London, being allocated to Stratford.

MR16 and MRL121 were the last MetroRiders to operate with Stagecoach East London. The majority were withdrawn during 1995, either being sold to Fleetmaster or cascaded to Stagecoach Western Scottish.

Under Stagecoach control a handful of MCW MetroRiders were loaned to Selkent, these operating in the striped livery. 2901 (F561HPP) was loaned from Stagecoach South, primarily for use on the 380 following a PVR increase. It is seen operating route 306 to Crystal Palace. *Ian Armstrong Collection*

October 1995 saw a handful of MetroRiders taken on loan from Stagecoach Busways, covering for Dennis Dart saloons that had moved to Bromley for the Christmas Park & Ride service. 1644 (E127KYW) originated with London Buses as MR27 and is seen in Orpington on its way to Green Street Green. *Ian Armstrong Collection*

London United

London United was privatised on 5 November 1994. At this time, four MCW MetroRiders were operated from Stamford Brook numbered MRL108/15-7. A number more were taken into stock from Westlink in September. These were numbered MR1-7, 10/1, 23, 30/1/4/9, 42/7, 52, 134 and MRL78-92. In April 1997 MRL78-80 were renumbered MRW2 to MRW4. These remained operating with London United until May 2000, at which time they departed the fleet.

Kentish Bus

Kentish Bus was the name of the former London Country (South East) operation. The company operated a number of MetroRiders, both MCW and Optare, some of which were used on London routes in south-east London. The first was the P14 (Surrey Quays–Isle of Dogs) in November 1988. For this route, a batch of MCW MetroRiders were purchased. These were late arriving, leading to five similar vehicles being hired from Northumbria Motor Services. Rolling stock numbers 804, 807-10 (E804/7-10BTN) were decorated in a red, white and blue Docklands Corporation livery. 807-10 were returned to Northumbria in December 1988, with 804 remaining with Kentish Bus until July 1992. The intended MetroRiders for the route arrived in December 1988; measuring 8.4m, they wore a similar livery to 804. Fleet numbers 860/1/3-5 were

Kentish Bus operated a number of London contracts in the late 1980s, early 1990s. One of these was the 42, typically operated by Dennis Dart saloons. It is seen on layover at Aldgate bus station showing off the cream and maroon livery worn by the Kentish Bus fleet. *Ian Armstrong Collection*

allocated to these vehicles which carried registration marks F860/1/3-5LCU. They later transferred to Londonlinks for use on services in Lewisham. 862 (F862LCU) arrived a little later in November 1989. It was put to use on routes in the Leyton and Lewisham areas. 887/9, 890 (H887/9/90OCU) arrived in January 1991, these being allocated to Northfleet for the B11.

Another MetroRider arrived in November 1995 numbered 865. It was initially loaned to Londonlinks before becoming a regular bus on the R5 (Orpington–Cudham–Knockholt–Orpington).

London & Country/Londonlinks

The MetroRider was not a common vehicle found in the London & Country fleet. Fourteen were purchased by the company for use on the 407 (Croydon–Caterham). They were numbered 440 to 453 (M440-53HPF) and arrived in October 1994. They operated with London & Country for four months before passing to a new company called Londonlinks in January 1995. Londonlinks was set up to deter competition between Kentish Bus and London & Country. The MetroRiders passed to Kentish Bus in 1996 when the Londonlinks operation was split between them and London & Country.

Fourteen Optare MetroRiders were purchased by London & Country in 1994, passing to Londonlinks in January 1995. They were taken into stock for use on the 407. 452 (M452HPG) is photographed in Sutton showing off the smart two-tone and red stripe livery. *Ian Armstrong Collection*

Capital Citybus

In March 1992 ten 8.4m Optare MetroRiders were acquired for route 236 (Finsbury Park Station–Hackney Wick). They also saw service on other midibus routes operated by the company. They were numbered 621 to 630 (J621-30HMH) and wore the distinctive all-yellow livery. Capital Citybus was later taken over by First Group on 8 July 1998, after which time a livery of red and yellow was introduced. In March 2001, they moved across to the W6 (Lower Edmonton–Southgate) for a short period of time. Two moved to Ponders End to support the fleet of Wright Handybus bodied Darts on the 462.

In April 2001, the company was successful in winning the contract for the 395 from Stagecoach London, this route running through the Rotherhithe Tunnel. MetroRiders were used on the service for a year before being replaced by new Mercedes-Benz Sprinters in April 2002.

Capital Citybus was another user of the MetroRider, with ten being taken into stock in the distinctive yellow livery. 623 (J623HMH) is captured by the camera at Southgate station on its way to Muswell Hill Broadway on the 299. *Ian Armstrong Collection*

R&I/MTL London/Metroline

R&I Coaches purchased three Optare MetroRiders for use on the Hampstead Hoppa services H1, H2 and H3. These were shorter than others that have been mentioned above, measuring 7.7m. A livery of red, grey and blue was worn by these vehicles until MTL London Northern took over the company, after which time they gained an all-red livery. Rolling stock numbers OM243/4 (M501/2ALP) and OM279 (P509NWU) were given to these saloons. London Northern was purchased by MTL Holdings on the 26 October 1994. These were not the first MetroRiders to operate with MTL London Northern. At the time of takeover, they were operating MRL210-22 from Holloway garage. In 1997, the company took stock of a pair of Optare MetroRiders to

MRL224 (P449SWX) was new to London Northern in 1997, being used on the W4. August 1998 saw the pair pass to Metroline. MRL224 is photographed wearing the later operator's livery whilst on layover at Golders Green bus station. *Ian Armstrong Collection*

OM279 (P509NWU) was one of three Optare MetroRiders new to R&I Tours, passing to MTL London Northern. They were inherited by Metroline in August 1998 and were used on the H1, H2 and H3 services in the Hampstead Garden Suburb area of north London. OM279 poses for the camera at Golders Green. *Ian Armstrong Collection*

cover an increase on the W4. Numbered MRL223 and MRL224, these vehicles carried registration marks P448/9SWX. They passed to Metroline in August 1998, retaining their fleet numbers. Metroline became the last operator in London to use the Optare MetroRider, with some originating with London Buses Limited being in stock and used on the W5. MRL243/4 were operated by Metroline until 2005 when they were replaced by Optare Solos.

F.E. Thorpe

Route C4 (Putney Pier–Hurlingham) was won by F.E. Thorpe in 1995. The route required small vehicles, with three MetroRiders being purchased, along with two second-hand MetroRiders. E134/5/7SNY were all sourced from Cardiff City Transport just before the route was taken over. They remained in use on the route until 1998, at which time they were replaced by newer Mercedes-Benz minibuses. They were supported by two former London Buses MetroRiders. MR54 (E930KYR) had operated with a couple of independent operators in Wales before passing to Thorpes in April 1995. D480PON, formerly MR20, was acquired from Metroline in January 1997. It was repainted red and yellow for use on the route.

Metrobus, Orpington

The MetroRider was first used by Metrobus on route 138 (Catford Bridge–Coney Hall) when it was taken on by the company in December 1995. The route had been previously operated by Londonlinks and Kentish Bus. The change of operator meant that Kentish Bus's MetroRiders 963 to 968 and 971/2 (J964-8, 971/2JNL) transferred to Metrobus.

A month later, in January 1996, six MetroRiders were taken into stock numbered 901 to 906 (N901-6HWY), these replacing the former Kentish Bus MetroRiders on the 138. After this time, they were put to further use on the 284 (Lewisham–Grove Park Cemetery) and 181 (Lewisham–Downham), both of which were taken over from Kentish Bus. Optare Excels replaced them in the autumn of 1996, after which time 963-8/71/2 were sold to Reading Buses and Guernseybus.

Another three MetroRiders were taken into stock by Metrobus in June 1997 when the business of East Surrey Buses was acquired. They took up rolling stock numbers 911, 917 and 918. 917 was first to be sold, passing to Guernseybus in March 2000.

The latter part of 1997 and January 1998 saw seven MetroRiders taken into stock from Stagecoach SelKent. Some were temporarily put to use on the 138 between February and June, whilst the Metrobus liveried MetroRiders were helping Stagecoach out on the C1 (Victoria Station–Kensington High Street). The route had been given up by London General in February 1998, and was being jointly operated by Stagecoach and Metrobus. Others were put to use on the former East Surrey routes. Some were withdrawn almost immediately in January 1998, the last few passing to Guernseybus in March 2000.

901-6 were replaced on the 138 in 2001 by low-floor Dennis Dart SLFs. It was soon found that the Dart SLF was more than capable of negotiating routes; the MetroRiders were placed into store.

Limebourne

Limebourne was set up by the Q-Drive group in March 1996 after they sold London Buslines and Berks Bucks Bus Co. to Centrewest. The contract for the C10 (Elephant & Castle–Victoria) was won by the company, starting in May 1996. For this, six Optare MetroRiders were leased by Limebourne. Registered N201-6MWW, they were numbered 2201 to 2206, operating from a base in Battersea. Route branding was carried by the MetroRiders. Limebourne entered receivership in 1998 with the MetroRiders returning off lease.

Epsom Buses

London General lost some contracts in October 1997, making some of their Optare MetroRiders surplus to requirement. MRL179-189 were acquired during October by Epsom Buses who repainted them into a cream and maroon livery. They lasted for just over a year, being replaced by Dennis Darts in January 1999. After this time, they found a new home with Reading Buses.

905 (N905HWY) was one of six Optare MetroRiders new to Metrobus in January 1996. It is seen on its way to Coney Hall on route 138 wearing the smart blue and yellow Metrobus livery. *Ian Armstrong Collection*

May 1996 saw six Optare MetroRiders enter the Limebourne fleet for the C10, the vehicles carrying route branding. 2202 (N202MWW) is seen at Victoria on its way to Elephant & Castle. *Mike Harris*

FREIGHT ROVER SHERPA

F reight Rover was created in 1981 as a subsidiary of the Land Rover Group. Under this new name a new brand was created for the vans built by British Leyland, introducing the Sherpa model. This was another model not taken into stock by London Buses in large numbers.

London Buses Limited

London Buses Limited took stock of a pair of Freight Rover Sherpa minibuses in April 1987, acquired from Carlyle of Birmingham. They were initially allocated to Bexleyheath where they were used on driver training duties. Fleet numbers SC1 and SC2 were allotted to the pair which carried registration marks D585OOV and D974PJW. In August 1991, these vehicles were put to use on the C1 in the Chelsea area.

Four Freight Rover Sherpas were loaned to London Buses in June 1989 for driver training duties, all being loaned from Carlyle, Birmingham. E968SVP was allocated to Orpington, whilst D118NON and F418/9BOP were allocated to Plumstead. These followed on from D262OOJ and D263OOJ which came from Ribble, the former vehicle again allocated to Orpington, the latter being allocated to Bexleyheath for driver training duties. D262OOJ and F419BOP were put to use on the 181 in July from Bexleyheath. The latter two Sherpas plus D118NON were reallocated to Plumstead in July for driver training duties.

F994XOV, a Carlyle bodied Freight Rover Sherpa demonstrator, arrived in August 1989. It was allocated to Bexleyheath. This was followed by D113, 121TFT in October. These found themselves operating from Orpington garage.

The final pair of Sherpas to be taken into stock by London Buses Limited arrived in June 1990, both being Dormobile bodied Sherpa 374s. D811KWT was sourced from West Riding, whilst D212GLJ came from Shamrock and Rambler. Numbered SD1 and SD2, both were allocated to Clapton for use on a contract for the Department of Health, running between Whitehall and Guy's Hospital. Both returned off lease in July 1991.

SC1 (D585OOV) was the only Sherpa to survive privatisation, being taken on by London General in November 1994. It was allocated to Putney garage and remained with the company until August 2000.

MERCEDES-BENZ 811D

The Mercedes-Benz 811D was one of a number of second-generation Mercedes-Benz commercial chassis introduced from 1986. It featured bodywork built by Alexander, Optare, Reeve Burgess, Crystals and Plaxton. It proved to be more popular with London operators than the 709D.

London Buses Limited

The first Mercedes-Benz 811Ds to enter service with London Buses carried the Optare StarRider bodywork. Demonstrator E95RWR was allocated to Orpington in February. The first of the type, SR1 (E711LYU), entered the fleet in June 1988, being used for training duties and publicity work. SR2 to SR4 (E712-4LYU) followed in July. These collectively entered service in November on the L3 between Downham and Catford.

The London Central division was the next recipient of the type. SR5 to SR28 (F905-28YWY) arrived in September (SR5-9), October (SR10-24) or November (SR25-8). All were allocated to Peckham for use on routes P11 (Waterloo Station–Peckham); P12 (Peckham Garage–Brockley) or P13 (Peckham Garage–Pepys Estate, Deptford). They gained Hoppa branding for use on these routes.

SR15 (F915YWY) formed part of the first batch of Mercedes-Benz 811Ds to operate with London Buses Limited. They were allocated to Peckham for three different services, one of these being the P11. *Ian Armstrong Collection*

The Alexander Sprint bodywork was the second type to enter service with London Buses Limited, becoming the MA-class. The first batch comprised 107 MAs, all of which were allocated to the Centrewest division. MA1, 2, 4-9, 10-4 arrived in October 1988 carrying registration marks F601XMS etc. They were joined in November by MA3, 10/6-35 (F603XMS etc). These 28-seaters were allocated to Westbourne Park where they displaced AEC Routemaster buses on routes 28 (Wandsworth–Golders Green) and 31 (Chelsea–Camden Town). The frequency on these two routes was doubled once the MAs had entered service. MA13 and MA14 were put to use from Victoria Basement on the C1, allowing London Buses Limited to evaluate longer midibuses on the route. MA12/6/7 and 24 were used at Uxbridge in December for driver training, with MA25 being allocated to Fulwell for this purpose. Others went to Uxbridge for driver familiarisation and training duties. MA38/9, 101/2/4/5 (F638/9, 701/2/4/5XMS) completed the 1988 deliveries, arriving in December.

A large influx of MA-class 811Ds, MA36/7 (F636/7XMS), MA54 (F694XMS), MA60-5, 93/5-9, 103 (F660-5XMS, F949/51-5BMS, F703XMS), arrived in January 1989. They were followed by MA40 to 53, 55-9, 66-81/3-92/4, 100/6/7 (F640-5, 695-9/90/1/4, 656-9/66-81/3-9XMS, F946-8/50BMS, F700/6/7XMS) in February. The final member of the first 107 of the type arrived in March numbered MA82 (F682XMS). Seventy-one of these (MA1-46/56-65/90-4/6-105) were allocated to Westbourne Park, completing the allocations on routes 28 and 31. Route 28 was converted in March 1989, with route 31 following in April. Vehicles on both routes wore Gold Arrow fleet names. Some of the batch mentioned above were renumbered in April so that the registrations matched fleet numbers. MA46-50 (F695-9XMS) became MA95-9; MA51-5 (F690-4XMS) were logically renumbered MA90-4. Others to be renumbered were MA90 to MA99 (F946-55BMS), which became MA46-55. MA20 went on loan to Selkent at Orpington in July, before returning to Westbourne Park in August.

Routes 28 and 31 were the first two routes to be operated by the Alexander bodied Mercedes-Benz 811D MA-class. MA19 (F619XMS) is photographed at Golders Green bus station prior to departing for Wandsworth on the 28. *Ian Armstrong*

Uxbridge finds
MA55 (F955BMS), seen having just completed its journey on the U2. As can be seen, these midibuses carried Uxbridge Buses branding. *Ian Armstrong Collection*

MA73 (F673XMS) was another 811D to be allocated to Uxbridge garage. It is seen heading towards Stockley on the U5. *Ian Armstrong Collection*

A third member of the Uxbridge allocation of MA-class 811Ds is MA86 (F686XMS). It is seen passing a Leyland National owned by The Beeline, completing its journey on the U3. *Ian Armstrong Collection*

MA47-55, 66-89, 95, 106/7 were allocated to Centrewest's Uxbridge garage from where they were used on a new network of local services which were branded as the U-Line. MA66 to MA80 were first to enter service, doing so in February 1989 on route U4 (Uxbridge Station–Hayes (Bourne Avenue)), this replacing route 204. The others entered service in May on routes U1 (Uxbridge Station–Ruislip Station); U2 (Uxbridge Station–Hillingdon Hospital/Oak Farm Estate); U3 (Uxbridge Station–West Drayton); U5 (Uxbridge Station–West Drayton Station). This new operation proved to be successful, and continued for many years after privatisation in 1994, with Uxbridge passing to Centrewest and later First London. MA45/6, 85/9 transferred from Uxbridge to Hanwell in May for use on the E5. A batch of MT-class 811Ds were due for the route but were late arriving. They soon returned to their home garage.

A large number of StarRiders also entered the fleet during 1989, with SR29-31 (F29-31CWY) arriving in January. SR29 was allocated to Plumstead to cover for the extension of route L3, whilst SR30/1 were allocated to Walthamstow. SR32-40 followed in February, being allocated to Victoria Basement. They were put to use on the C1 and C2, replacing Ivecos E291-6VOM, which were returned off lease. These were joined by SR41 and SR42 in March, these carrying registration marks F41/2CWY. SR41 went to Victoria Basement, whilst SR42 was allocated to Walthamstow. It was joined there in May by SR43/9-53 (F43/9-53CWY), all of which were put to use on the 211 between Waltham Cross and Breach Barns. SR41 transferred to Walthamstow in June, operating alongside this batch on the 211. SR44 to SR48 (F44-8CWY) filled the gap, operating route 286 (Greenwich, Cutty Sark–Eltham) from New Cross.

SR36 (F36CWY) was one of nine 811Ds allocated to Victoria Basement for the C1 and C2. It is seen waiting to start its journey on the latter route to Oxford Circus. *Ian Armstrong Collection*

Stanmore Underground station finds SR95 (G95KUB). It is seen having completed its journey on route H12. By the time the SR-class were allocated to North Wembley, the Harrow Buses livery had been eradicated, being replaced by the simple Harrow Buses name as seen on the front of SR95. *Ian Armstrong Collection*

SR54-9 (F154-9FWY) arrived in July; allocated to Bexleyheath, they wore a blue and cream livery and operated under the Bexleybus name, a low-cost bus unit set up in the Bexleyheath area by London Buses Limited. They were mostly used on the B16 (Ferrier Estate–Bexleyheath) and carried local fleet numbers 108 to 113.

SR60 to SR64 (F160-4FWY) preceded the Bexleybus fleet, arriving in June. SR60 was loaned to Orpington, transferring a month later to Catford. The latter garage became home to SR61-4. These were joined in July by SR65 to SR79 (F165-79FWY), and SR80/1 (F180/1FWY) in August. SR61-81 were collectively used on the 160 (Catford, St Dunstan's College–Eltham–Southend Crescent).

The next twenty-four were destined for the Harrow area. Prior to their arrival, an Optare StarRider bodied Mercedes-Benz 811D registered F479FUA was loaned to North Wembley for driver training duties. The first two, SR82/3 (G82/3KUB), arrived at North Wembley in August. They were followed by SR84 to SR94 (G84-94KUB) in September. SR95-104 (G95-104KUB) arrived in October, and the batch was complete in November when SR105 (G105KUB) put in an appearance. They were put to use on the H11 to H15 group of services, displacing older MCW MetroRiders on these routes. They wore an all-red livery, being given either Harrow Buses or Harrow Hoppa fleet names.

The 1989 deliveries were completed in November (SR106 to SR120 – G106-20KUB) and December (SR121 – G121KUB) when these vehicles arrived at Victoria Basement. They were used to replace some of the OV-class Optare CityPacers.

A fleet of six Reeve Burgess bodied Mercedes-Benz minibuses were taken into stock during 1989. All but one of these were of the 709D model. However, the sixth member of the batch, MT6 (F396DHL), was an 811D. Measuring 8.4m, this midibus arrived in January and was allocated to the SelKent operation for use on the private hire Selkent Travel operation. MT6 was used by London Buses for both private hire and driver training duties. Allocated to Catford, it soon gained private registration mark VLT77.

Two longer Reeve Burgess bodied 811Ds were taken into stock by London Buses during November. Numbered MTL1 and MTL2 (G621XLO, G622KWE), the first was allocated to Uxbridge for use on the U-Line routes, working alongside the MA-class 811Ds. MTL2 went to Westbourne Park, initially on lease before being officially acquired in 1990, at which time it moved to Victoria Basement.

Another body builder to produce bodywork for the Mercedes-Benz 811D was Wrightbus of Ballymena, Northern Ireland. The first sixteen arrived over the course of November and December 1989. Numbered MW1 to MW16, they carried Northern Irish registration marks HDZ2601-16. They worked alongside SR-class StarRiders on midibus routes 108B (Crystal Palace–Lewisham–Surrey Docks); 160 (Catford, St Dunstan's College–Eltham, Southend Crescent); 181 (Lewisham–Downham); 225 (Lewisham–Rotherhithe), 273 (Lewisham Tesco–Grove Park Station) and 284 (Lewisham–Grove Park Station). MW2, 8 and 14 were fitted with wheelchair lifts for use on Mobility Services.

SR122 and SR123 (G122/3SMV) were the final Optare StarRiders to be purchased by London Buses Limited. These arrived in January 1990 and were allocated to London Central at Peckham, replacing the two that had been diverted to New Cross for the 286 route. In September 1990, several SRs moved around London Buses. At this time SR10, 15 and 19 moved to Peckham; whilst SR56, 57 and 71 moved from Bexleyheath to Catford. Soon after transfer, SR10 caught fire whilst in service in Waterloo. It was subsequently cannibalised at Peckham before being scrapped.

East London was successful in gaining the contract for the S2 (Lea Valley Ice Centre–Stratford). This required seven midibuses, for which SR31, 41-3, 49 and 52/3 moved

MTL2 (G222KWE) was one of two longer Reeve Burgess bodied 811Ds purchased by London Buses. It was allocated to Westbourne Park and was used alongside the MA-class on the 28. *Ian Armstrong Collection*

MW7 (HDZ2607) was one of sixteen Wright bodied 811Ds allocated to Catford in the winter of 1989. It is seen on its way to Catford. *Mike Harris*

from Walthamstow to Bow in February 1990. However, these did not last long, being replaced by RB-class Renault midibuses in November. After this they moved on to London Central at Camberwell for use on the P5 (Elephant & Castle–Brixton), being branded as the 'Camberwell Clipper'.

A Dormobile bodied 811D arrived in March 1990 at North Wembley. Registered G590PKL, this vehicle operated with Metroline for two weeks on routes H14 and H15. However, no orders were placed for this combination.

MA108 to MA124 (G108-24PGT) were next to arrive, doing so in April 1990. They were allocated to London General's Victoria Basement for use on the 239 (Victoria Station–Clapham Junction). They gained Streetline branding for use on the route.

Two additional demonstrators were used for a short period by London Buses during 1990. A Whittaker bodied 811D arrived in April. Registered G395OWB, it gained temporary fleet number ME1. It was initially allocated to Victoria Basement but was not used from there. In August it transferred to Walthamstow where it was used in service. The second arrived in June 1990 carrying a PMT body. G495FFA was put to use from Potters Bar on route 384 (Cockfosters Station–Barnet Station) from August. The same month, it went on loan to County Bus before returning to London Buses in August, being allocated to Orpington upon its return. No further orders were placed in the London area for either bodywork.

Three additional Reeve Burgess bodied 811Ds arrived with London Buses in November 1990. These carried on from the previous year's deliveries as MTL3 to MTL5 (H189/91/2RWF). They were allocated one apiece to Orpington, Victoria and Westbourne Park, later moving to Catford, Peckham and Victoria. The trio moved around London Buses as required, filling in gaps for larger midibuses.

Another body style, manufactured by Carlyle, was introduced to the London Buses fleet in 1990, mounted on the Mercedes-Benz 811D chassis. Registered F430BOP, this

SR41 (F41CWY) moved to Camberwell in November for use on the P5. It is photographed whilst loading at Elephant & Castle. *Ian Armstrong Collection*

Seventeen MA-class 811DS were allocated to Victoria Basement for route 239. The penultimate member of the batch, MA123 (G123PGT), is seen passing Victoria Coach Station on its way to Clapham Junction. The Streetline branding applied to these vehicles can be seen on the front and sides. *Ian Armstrong Collection*

vehicle took up rolling stock number MC1 and was allocated to Selkent at Catford. MC1 was formerly a demonstration vehicle and had previously operated with London Buses from Croydon in July and August 1989, being used on the 254 at this time. Four additional Carlyle bodied 811Ds arrived in August. They continued the numbering sequence as MC2 to MC5, registered H882-5LOX. They were allocated to Orpington for use on Roundabout route R3.

Wright bodied 811D demonstrator IDZ8561 arrived in November 1990. It was allocated rolling stock number MW00 and was initially used from Bow before moving on to Walthamstow, North Wembley, Peckham and Putney.

The MA-class fell victim to their own success, becoming too small to cope with the demand. Wright Handybus bodied Dennis Dart saloons replaced the MAs on route 31 in February 1991, with those on the 28 soon following. This left a large number of MAs surplus to requirements, which led to many being moved around London Buses. In April, MA34-9, 95 and 105 were transferred to Hanwell for use on the 195 (Charville Lane Estate–Ealing Hospital), which had been won from London Buslines. For this they lost their Gold Arrow branding in favour of Midilink branding. MA80/1 moved to Uxbridge in August to take up service on Hertfordshire County Council funded service R1, linking Uxbridge with Chorleywood, Rickmansworth and Harefield. A month later, Alperton took some of the surplus MAs to convert route 224 (Willesden Junction Station–North Wembley) to the type. Some remained at Westbourne Park for the take up of route 70 (Kensington–Acton). MA9, 14-7/9-21/4/5/9, 30/1, 41 transferred south of the river, being reallocated to Selkent. Four of these joined the general midibus pool at Bromley, with two others being allocated to Catford. The remaining MAs were allocated to Plumstead for use on the 202 (Blackheath–Catford).

The final nine MA-class 811Ds arrived in May 1991, continuing on from the Victoria Basement batch, taking stock numbers MA125-34 along with registration marks H425-34XGK. They were allocated to London General's Putney garage from where they operated the 39. Like the previous MAs, these vehicles also carried Streetline branding.

MT6 transferred across to Plumstead in January 1991, and in June of this year it was re-numbered MTL6. MTL3 went to Penzance in March 1991 to help with a recruitment drive taking place in that area at that time. Returning in July, it moved to Bexleyheath, joined there by MTL1, 2 and 4, and worked alongside the RB-class. MTL3 made the same journey south-east in 1992. MTL5 continued operating as and where it was needed. Being used at Bexleyheath, Catford, Potters Bar, Greenford and Alperton, it finally settled at the latter garage for a while.

After heavy tender losses in the Harrow area, the Harrow Buses operation was closed in January 1991. This meant that the majority of StarRiders used from North Wembley were no longer required. Those routes retained were operated by Metroline using DT-class Darts. At this time SR50, 86 and 101 transferred to Selkent at Catford; SR51 moved to London Central at Peckham. East London took stock of SR90 and SR96, allocating them to Bow. SR82/3/7/8, 92/8, 100/3/4 were transferred from North Wembley to nearby Edgware. These were put to use on the 143 (Brent Cross–Archway Station), gaining Skipper branding. SR84/5, 91/3-5/7/9, 102/5 moved to London Northern at Potters Bar. From there they were used on two new midibus routes, one of which was the 326 (Hendon Central–New Barnet/Potters Bar). For the route they gained Midilink branding. SR54/5/7/8/9, 61/7/8 moved from London Central to Edgware in October 1991 where they displaced DT-class Darts which moved on to North Wembley.

MC3 (H883LOX) was one of five Carlyle bodied Mercedes-Benz 811Ds to be allocated to the Roundabout operation in Orpington. It is seen in Orpington heading towards Petts Wood Station on the R3. *Ian Armstrong Collection*

The R3 was the recipient of the five MC-class 811Ds. Orpington town centre finds MC5 (H885LOX), seen on its way to Green Street Green. *Ian Armstrong Collection*

MA61 (F661XMS) was one of the MA-class 811Ds to move from Westbourne Park to Hanwell for use on services in the Ealing and Greenford area. It is seen operating route 282 to Ealing Hospital. *Ian Armstrong Collection*

MA17 (F617XMS) transferred south of the river after being replaced from routes 28 and 31. It is seen heading towards Greenwich Hospital on route 386. *Ian Armstrong Collection*

MA21 (F621XMS) was another MA-class midibus to move south of the river to Plumstead. It is seen in Lewisham, heading towards West Croydon on the 54. *Ian Armstrong Collection*

Nine MA-class
811Ds were allocated
to London General's
garage at Putney in
May 1991 for use on
the 39. However,
they were also used
on other services
from the garage.
MA128 (H428XGK)
is photographed
at Putney Bridge
Underground station
on route 265.
Matthew Wharmby

MC1 was returned to Carlyle for refurbishment in June 1991 and to cover for its absence, similar H727LOL came on loan from Carlyle, being allocated to Orpington.

It wasn't until 1992 that the next Wright bodied 811D arrived with London Buses, beginning with MW17 (LDZ9017) which was allocated to West Ham in July. MW17 stood out from other 811Ds in the fleet, featuring a sloped front end. It soon moved to Victoria Basement, remaining there until March 1994 when it transferred to Greenford.

Optare StarRider bodied 811D SR1 was re-registered from E711LYU to WLT461 in February. SR5-9, 12/3/5/7/8, 20 (F905-9/12/3/5/7/8/20YWY) moved from Stockwell to Norwood between August and October 1992. They entered service on the 322 (Crystal Palace–Vauxhall Station) and gained Connexions branding.

The final twenty Wright bodied 811Ds arrived in April and May 1993. MW18 to MW37 (NDZ7918-37) were allocated to London Northern at Potters Bar where they were branded as Midilink. They were used on midibus routes in the Barnet area.

The summer of 1993 saw MA3 to MA7 sent north to South Yorkshire Transport for the fitment of wheelchair lifts. These were fitted to the front doorways instead of the rear like the MT-class. They gained Southall Shuttle livery and replaced MT1-4 on the E5 (Greenford–Havelock Estate).

Cricklewood received a small batch of StarRiders in the latter part of 1993, these being transferred from Victoria and Potters Bar. Bromley also received a small fleet of SRs at this time for use on the 396 (Eltham–Bromley).

Holloway received SR35-40 and 106-121 after the C2 moved to this garage from Victoria Basement which was closed in January 1994. SR1 lost its cherished registration mark WLT461 in favour of new mark E155CGJ in March 1994. The loss of routes by Selkent in south-east London to Kentish Bus meant that a number of StarRiders moved to East London for RB-class replacement at Bow. Edgware re-opened as a garage in February 1994, leading to the transfer of SR7/8, 12, 54/5/7-9, 61/7/8, 76-9,

SR100 (G100KUB) moved from North Wembley to Edgware following the closure of the Harrow Bus operation in January 1991. It is photographed at Edgware bus station branded as Skipper. *Ian Armstrong Collection*

Other SRs displaced from the Harrow Buses operation moved to nearby Potters Bar. SR93 (G93KUB) was one of these and is seen operating the 384 to Barnet. Midilink branding was applied to these buses. *Ian Armstrong Collection*

81-5/7-90/2-6/8, 100/1/3/4/5 from Cricklewood. Just prior to privatisation, route C2 gained a fleet of new Northern Counties bodied Dennis Darts. These replaced the StarRiders, with SR33-8, 40 moving across to Enfield in June for use on the 192 (Enfield Town–Angel Road Tesco).

MW37 lost its Northern Irish registration mark (NDZ7937) in January 1994 in favour of new mark K476FYN. The same fate was experienced by MW36 in February when it gained new registration mark K510FWN. MW2, 8 and 14 gained a red and yellow Mobility bus livery in March.

MW17 (LDZ9017) stood out from other MWs in the London Buses fleet, featuring a sloped front. Operating from West Ham and Victoria Basement, it moved to Greenford in early 1994. Whilst based at this garage it gained Challenger fleet names. It is seen departing Heathrow Central bus station at the start of its journey to Greenford Station. *Jeff Lloyd*

SR12 (F912YWY) moved to Norwood garage from Stockwell in September 1992. It was placed into service on the 322 from its new garage, gaining Connexions branding. It is seen approaching journey's end at Crystal Palace. *Ian Armstrong Collection*

MW20 (NDZ7920) represents the last batch of MW-class 811Ds to enter service with London Buses. These were allocated to Potters Bar for use on routes in the Barnet area. Midilink branding was applied to this batch of vehicles. *Ian Armstrong Collection*

MA3-7 were fitted with wheelchair lifts and gained the deep cream waistband for use on the E5 in 1993. These were used to replace the MT-class midibuses. MA7 (F607XMS) is photographed in Greenford on route E5. *Ian Armstrong Collection*

Crystals

Crystals of Dartford purchased a pair of Optare StarRiders in 1988 for use on the 146 (Bromley North–Downe). These vehicles were registered E281TWW and E456VUM.

The company won the contracts for Orpington routes R2 and R8 from Stagecoach London and Kentish Bus in 1996. For these routes they ordered six Mercedes-Benz 811Ds, bodied by Crystals. Registered N601-6JGP, these vehicles arrived with the company in December 1995. They operated with Crystals until being sold in 2002/2003.

Eastern National Citybus/Thamesway

Eastern National was the next operator to take stock of the Mercedes-Benz 811D chassis, this time carrying Reeve Burgess bodywork. Route W13 required longer midibuses, resulting in the company purchasing 0800 to 0804 (F800-4RHK), which arrived in March 1989.

Seven Plaxton Beaver bodied Mercedes-Benz 811Ds were purchased by Thamesway in October 1992 for use on the D8. Registered K805-11DJN, they were numbered 0805-0811. However, these were late arriving and older Beavers filled the gap until their arrival. By this time, Eastern National had changed the name of their London operations to Thamesway.

1996 saw the contracts for routes R2 and R8 taken over by Crystals of Dartford. For the route six Mercedes-Benz 811Ds were purchased. The third member of the batch, N603JGP, is seen on layover at Petts Wood Station. *Ian Armstrong Collection*

The Isle of Dogs finds First Thamesway's 808 (K808DJN) seen operating the D8. *Matthew Wharmby*

Sovereign, Harrow

Sovereign Bus and Coach was formed in January 1989 when the former London Country (North East) operation was split into two. Sovereign took responsibility for garages at St Albans, Hatfield and Stevenage. The company was successful in winning four LRT contracts in the Harrow area of North London in 1990, most of which started in early 1991. Two of these, the H10 (Harrow circular) and H17 (Harrow–Vale Farm, Sudbury), required slightly larger midibuses, with seventeen Reeve Burgess bodied Mercedes-Benz 811Ds being ordered for the two routes. These duly arrived in November 1990, carrying registration marks H403/4/6-11/3/5/7-9/21-4FGS.

H418FGS was one of seventeen Mercedes-Benz 811Ds with Reeve Burgess bodywork that were used on local services in the Harrow area. It is photographed on layover at Harrow bus station. *Ian Armstrong Collection*

H423FGS was the penultimate member of the seventeen strong batch of 811Ds to operate with Sovereign Harrow. It is seen loading at Harrow bus station. *Ian Armstrong Collection*

They remained operating in the Harrow area for the majority of time the contract was operated by Sovereign. In 1993, fleet numbers were added to the vehicles, these matching the numbers in the registration marks. 455 to 461 (M455-61UUR) were earmarked for the Harrow operation, but these soon moved to other Sovereign operations as required. An influx of new Plaxton Pointer bodied Dart SLFs in 1999 caused the withdrawal and sale of the 811Ds from Sovereign.

County Bus

The other part of the former London Country (North East) operation was named County Bus and Coach. This operation took stock of twelve Reeve Burgess bodied 811Ds in 1991 ready for the take up of LRT route W15 in the Walthamstow area. MD601 to MD612 (J601-12WHJ) carried twenty-eight seats and were allocated to a new garage set up in Gibbs Road, Edmonton. All twelve midibuses carried the Lea Valley banner. Like other midibuses in London, little happened to this modest batch during their working lives in London.

County Bus came under the ownership of Arriva in 1997, being owned by the Cowie Group prior to this. A re-organisation of Arriva's operations in London and the Home Counties meant that control of Edmonton garage, along with the forty-seven buses allocated to it, transferred from Arriva East Herts & Essex, as County Bus had become known, to Arriva London North. With the exception of MD602, which had been written off after an accident and suffered fire damage in February 1998, the other MD-class 811Ds transferred to the new owner.

London Buslines

London Buslines purchased a fleet of Reeve Burgess Beaver bodied Mercedes-Benz 811Ds for routes 201 (Hounslow–Staines) and 203 (Hounslow–Hatton Cross–Staines) in August 1991. However, the new buses were not ready in time, leading to the company hiring six Dodge S75 midibuses to cover until the intended fleet arrived in October. Carrying 28-seater bodies, these vehicles were numbered 631/2/4-7 (J31/2/4-7KLR).

The 201 was withdrawn in November 1993, the displaced 811Ds being used to strengthen route 203. Centrewest purchased London Buslines from Q-Drive in 1996. The contract for the 203 was renewed by the company, but the rolling stock was replaced by new Plaxton Pointer bodied Dennis Dart saloons. The 811Ds transferred to The Beeline at Slough during 1996.

Hatton Cross finds London Buslines 632 (J32KLR). It is seen loading at Hatton Cross on its way to Staines on route 201. *Ian Armstrong Collection*

637 (J37KLR) also represents the small batch of 811Ds operated by London Buslines. It is seen operating the C4 when photographed on Harwood Road. *Mike Harris*

R&I Tours

R&I Tours of Acton acquired a pair of Optare StarRider bodied Mercedes-Benz 811Ds from Reading Buses in November 1991. Numbered 230 and 231 (F607/8SDP), they were used on routes C11 (Brent Cross–Archway) and C12 (King's Cross–Finchley Road Station). They remained in the fleet until April 1995, at which time they were sold.

Capital Citybus

Capital Citybus was successful in winning a number of LRT contracts at the expense of London Buses' Tottenham garage, all starting in February 1992. Twenty 811Ds, complete with Reeve Burgess Beaver bodies, were purchased. All arrived in January 1992, taking up rolling stock numbers 601 to 620 (J601HMF etc). Six routes in total were won, these being the 153 (Finsbury Park–Smithfield); 298 (Southgate Station–South Mimms); 299 (Muswell Hill Broadway–Southgate Station–Cockfosters); W6 (Southgate–Lower Edmonton) and W10 (Crews Hill Station–Clay Hill–Chase Side–Enfield Town). Routes D4 (Leamouth–Mile End) and 236 (Finsbury Park Station–Hackney Wick) were also won, for which additional midibuses were ordered. Five (603/4/7-9) left the fleet in January and February 1994, being sold to Citibus Tours of Oldham.

Three Alexander bodied 811Ds with Capital Citybus arrived in April 1992. Numbered 631 to 633 (J631-3HMH), they were used on route D4. The trio were late arriving, leading to the loan of three Carlyle bodied 811Ds from Red Admiral of Portsmouth. Registered H985/8/9FTT, they operated on these routes until the intended rolling stock arrived.

610 (J610HMF) was first to receive the red and yellow Capital Citybus 80 per cent red livery. By this time, it was primarily being used on route 318 between Stamford Hill and North Middlesex Hospital.

612 (J612HMF) is seen at the Finsbury Park terminus of route 153. It is seen wearing the original yellow livery used by Capital Citybus. *Ian Armstrong Collection*

Twelve of the fleet carried on operating through the First Group takeover in July 1998. They were joined by former First Thamesway 811Ds 800 to 804 (F800-4RHK) when the latter operator's Ponders End garage transferred to the control of First Capital. These gained rolling stock numbers 600/6/7/3/4.

The remaining 811Ds were sold in January and February 2001, passing to First Mainline, operating in the Rotherham area of South Yorkshire.

616 (J616HMF) was another of the 20-strong batch of Mercedes-Benz 811Ds operated by Capital Citybus. It is captured by the camera at Southgate station before heading towards South Mimms on the 298. *Ian Armstrong Collection*

610 (J610HMF) was the first 811D in the Capital Citybus fleet to gain the 80 per cent red livery. It is seen operating route 318 to Stamford Hill. *Ian Armstrong Collection*

Transcity

Three Dormobile bodied 811Ds with Transcity arrived in January 1993; registered K981-3KGY they were put to use on route B15, although they could be found operating other routes.

Docklands Transit

Docklands Transit was part of the Transit Holdings Group. From 20 March 1993 the company commenced operation of routes 287 (Barking–Rainham); 366 (Barking–Leytonstone) and 368 (Barking–Chadwell Heath). Twenty-one Carlyle bodied Mercedes-Benz 811Ds were acquired from both Red Admiral, Portsmouth and Thames Transit, Oxford. The vehicles acquired were numbered 367/8/70/1 (H985/6/8/9FTT); 389 (H180GTA); 390/3/4/5/8/9 (H781/4/5/6/9/90GTA); 400-9 (H101-10HDV). 389/90/3/4/5/8 were those acquired from Red Admiral, the others being sourced from Thames Transit. 367/70/1 had been on loan to Capital Citybus during February 1992. An additional 811D (2010 – K711UTT) was inspected by Docklands Transit but was rejected by the company. 408 (H109HDV) was written off by the company in September 1996 after suffering an electrical fire.

The Stagecoach Group purchased the operations of Transit Holdings Ltd on 22 July 1997. After this time, Docklands Transit was added to the Stagecoach East London operation. 367-71 H985-9FTT; 389/90 H180, 781GTA; 393-5/8/9 H784-6/9/90GTA; 400-7/9 H101-8/10HDV were briefly used by Stagecoach East London whilst eighteen Plaxton Pointer bodied Dennis Darts were delivered.

Docklands Transit operated twenty-one Carlyle bodied Mercedes-Benz 811D midibuses on three services in north-east London. 370 (H988FTT) is seen on the 287 heading towards Barking. *Ian Armstrong Collection*

H985FTT is photographed at Southgate station on route 298 to South Mimms. It is seen carrying Red Admiral fleet names. *Ian Armstrong Collection*

390 (H781GTA) was acquired by Docklands Transit from Red Admiral. It is seen on its way to Redbridge whilst operating the 366. *Ian Armstrong Collection*

H103HDV was sourced from Thames Transit, Oxford and was numbered 402 by Docklands Transit. It is seen on layover in Barking whilst operating route 366. *Ian Armstrong Collection*

London & Country/Londonlinks

London & Country took stock of eight Plaxton Beaver bodied 811Ds in March 1994 for route 367 (Bromley North–West Croydon). These vehicles were numbered 430 to 437 by the company, carrying registration marks L430-7CPJ. In January 1995 the route and vehicles transferred to the newly formed Londonlinks operation, later becoming known as Arriva Croydon and North Surrey. 432 was destroyed by fire in November 1995, and was replaced by a new vehicle numbered 438 (P438HKN), later becoming MM438.

436 (L436CPJ) was the penultimate member of an eight-strong batch of Mercedes-Benz 811D midibuses operated by London & Country on route 367. It shows off the smart two-tone green and red livery worn by the London & Country, and Londonlinks, operations. *Ian Armstrong Collection*

Centrewest/First London

At the time of privatisation, 2 September 1994, the majority of the MA-class 811Ds (MA1-8, 10-3, 18, 22/3/6-8, 32-40/2-107) passed to Centrewest's ownership. The company won contracts in the Oprington area from Selkent in 1995. After these wins, MA58 was transferred to Orpington in June for driver training and route learning. MA13, 18, 22, 27 and 33 also transferred south-east in November 1995, being allocated to the newly opened Swanley garage, from where they were used on the R3 and R4, covering for the late arrival of new rolling stock. They returned to Greenford in January 1996.

A solitary Reeve Burgess bodied 811D was also transferred from London Buses Limited in 1994, this being MTL5 (H192RWF). Joining other MAs at Orpington for a short period of time whilst new midibuses were awaited. They also took stock of Wright bodied 811D MW17 at this time, this vehicle was allocated to Greenford.

April 1996 saw the loss of routes 95 and 105 at Alperton. At this time, MA11, 32/4/7/9, 90-4/7/8, 100/2/3/5 all transferred across to Greenford where they replaced RW-class Renault minibuses.

Former London Buslines 631-4 (J31-4KLR) were loaned to Swanley from the Bee Line, Slough in 1996, along with London Buslines owned 636 (J36KLR). These came on loan in time for the 1996 Bromley Park & Ride service.

The introduction of low-floor Dennis Darts during 1997 meant that a number of MA-class midibuses left Centrewest for new homes with Eastern Counties and Strathclyde Buses. The last members of the MA-class, with the exception of MA1, passed to First Western National during October 1998. MA1 (F601XMS) was retained by Centrewest for preservation. It later passed to the London Transport Museum.

Centrewest purchased ten Marshall bodied Mercedes-Benz 811Ds for use in the Orpington area. MM1 to MM7 (N521-7MEW) were new in December 1995. Allocated to Swanley garage, they were used on the R3 and R4. However, they could be found operating on any of Orpington's routes, as could the Dennis Dart saloons allocated to Swanley. In March 1996, a new garage opened at Faraday Road, St Mary Cray, replacing

MM3 (N523REW) was one of ten Marshall bodied 811Ds to be purchased by Centrewest for use in Orpington. It is seen at Bromley North operating the 336 to Locks Bottom, displaying Orpington Buses fleet names. *Ian Armstrong Collection*

Swanley as the base for the Orpington operations. In August, the remaining three Marshall bodied 811Ds were taken into stock numbered MM8 to MM10 (P488-90CEG). They were put to use on the 336 (Locks Bottom–Bromley North Station). All ten remained operating in London until November 1999, at which time they passed to First Leicester.

Stagecoach London

Stagecoach purchased the operations of East London and Selkent on 6 September 1994. At the time of takeover, a number of MA-class 811Ds were being operated by the company from Plumstead. These were numbered MA9, 14-7/9-21/4/5/9, 30/1 and 41 and were mostly used on the 202. The introduction of new Alexander Dash bodied Dennis Darts on the route in 1996 meant that the fleet was withdrawn, passing to sister companies Stagecoach Cleveland Transit, Stagecoach Devon or Stagecoach Bluebird.

The MAs were joined by MTL6 (VLT77). It operated briefly with Stagecoach Selkent before moving on to Stagecoach Fife Scottish in November 1994 for further use.

A larger number of Optare StarRider bodied 811Ds were being operated by East London at the time of privatisation. SR1-4, 12/3, 32, 50/6, 60/5/6/9, 70-80, 86, 91, 105-7, 119 were shared between Upton Park and Stratford garages.

Stagecoach Selkent also acquired the fleet of five Carlyle bodied 811Ds, MC1 to MC5. All were allocated to Orpington for use on the Roundabout network.

Despite the ten Marshall bodied 811Ds being purchased for use on Orpington area services R3 and R4, they were often found on the 336. Just like MM3 in the previous photograph, MM9 (P489CEG) is also found on this latter service. It is captured by the camera in Bromley town centre. *Ian Armstrong Collection*

Stagecoach Selkent were also using MW1-16 at the time of privatisation from Catford. The first (MW1/3-7, 10-2/6) left London in December 1995, passing to Stagecoach Cleveland Transit. Others left the capital in 1996. However, MW2, 8 and 14 were retained for use on mobility routes until April 1997, at which time they passed to Stagecoach owned Circle Line.

MC1 lost its cherished registration mark WLT491 in July 1995 in favour of F286KGK. At the same time, MC4 lost registration mark WLT400, being re-registered H509AGC. The loss of the Orpington operation to Centrewest in November 1995 saw MC1-5 transfer to Catford before being sold to Stagecoach Fife Scottish the same month.

Several rail replacement bus services were operated in East London, replacing the East London Line. One service, commencing in March 1995, required a fleet of nineteen Optare StarRiders. For this route, Stagecoach East London painted seventeen SRs (SR12, 13, 32, 50, 56, 60, 70, 72, 73, 74, 75, 76, 80, 91, 105, 106, 107) into an orange and white livery for the route. They moved south to Selkent at Catford, from where the route was operated. SR32, 60, 75, 80 and 106 moved north again in May 1995, to Stratford.

The majority of Stagecoach's SRs left London between 1996 and 1998. A problem with low-floor Dart SLFs accessing part of route 284 (Lewisham–Grove Park Cemetery) resulted in a couple of SRs being retained for a little longer whilst the problems were sorted. This led to the introduction of temporary route 584 (Lewisham–Catford). SR106 was one of those retained for the route, remaining operational with Stagecoach until July 2001, after which time it was sold.

As mentioned above, on 22 July 1997, the Stagecoach Group acquired the operations of Transit Holdings Ltd. This included the operations of Docklands Transit who were operating a number of routes centred on the Barking area of

SR12 (E712LYU) was part of a large batch of SR-class Optare StarRider bodied Mercedes-Benz 811Ds to transfer to the ownership of Stagecoach East London in September 1994. It is seen displaying the logos of its new owner. *Ian Armstrong Collection*

SR105 (G105KUB)
was one of a number
of Optare StarRider
bodied 811Ds to be
used by Stagecoach
London on the
East London Line
rail replacement.
It is captured by
the camera at
Whitechapel Station.
Mike Harris

East London. Eighteen Plaxton Pointer bodied Dennis Darts were in the process of delivery to replace a number of 811Ds with Docklands Transit. Whilst these were delivered, 367-71 H985-9FTT; 389/90 H180, 781GTA; 393-5/8/9 H784-6/9/90GTA and 400-7/9 H101-8/10HDV were taken into stock for a short period. Once the Darts had arrived, the 811Ds departed for new lives with Stagecoach Western Scottish and Stagecoach Bluebird.

London Central/London General/
Go Ahead London

London General was the only other former London Buses operation to take stock of the MA-class 811D post-privatisation. On 2 November 1994 MA108 to MA134 passed to the new operation, being shared between Battersea Minibus base and Putney. Little of interest happened to this fleet of vehicles for their careers with the company.

London Central took stock of MTL1 to MTL4 from London Buses Limited on 22 September 1994, these being allocated to Bexleyheath garage. They remained operational with London Central until July 1995; at which time they were sold to the Wycombe Bus Company.

SR11/4/6/9, 21-31, 41-3/5/7/8/9, 51-3, 62/3, 122/3 were also operating with London Central at the time of privatisation. These were shared between Peckham, Camberwell and Bexleyheath. As with other operators post-privatisation, the SRs hung

MA115 (G115PGT) was one of a number of 811Ds to be taken over by London General at the time of privatisation. They retained the Streetline branding. It is seen at Elephant & Castle whilst on its way to Clapham Junction on route 344. *Ian Armstrong Collection*

on for a number of years with London Central. The majority of them left the fleet during 1998. SR31 and 41 transferred to sister Go-Ahead operator Metrobus of Orpington.

From 23 May 1996, London General came under the ownership of the Go-Ahead Group, who also owned London Central. In May 1996 MA109-12/5-20/7 left London for further service with sister Go-Ahead operation Wycombe Bus Company. In December 1996, MA110/4/5, 123/9 transferred to London Central at Camberwell. They worked alongside Dennis Darts on route 484 (Lewisham–Camberwell Green), helping to cover for an increase in the PVR. MA121 joined them in March 1997. These were eventually sold to MK Metro, Milton Keynes, the last of which leaving London in the spring of 1998.

Leaside Buses/South London/Arriva London

At the time of privatisation, 29 September 1994, SR33-8, 40 were operating route 192 from Leaside's Enfield garage. They remained operating with Leaside Buses until the spring of 1996 when they were sold to Fleetmaster of Horsham.

South London was the last of the former London Buses Limited operations to be privatised, this being completed in January 1995. At this time, SR5/6/9, 15/7/8, 20, 39, 46, 97, 99, 102 passed to the new operator, all being allocated to Norwood. The introduction of Dennis Darts at Thornton Heath led to the transfer of SR5, 9, 39 and 99 to Leaside Buses at Enfield, replacing similar vehicles. SR34/7/8 were also transferred but were withdrawn and sold to Fleetmaster in January 1996.

As mentioned above, a re-organisation of the Arriva operations in London and the Home Counties meant that a fleet of Reeve Burgess bodied 811Ds transferred from

Arriva East Herts & Essex in October 1997. These retained their former operators' fleet numbers MD601/3-12 (J601/3-12WHJ), all of which continued operating the W15 from Edmonton.

Another re-organisation on 30 October 1999 saw the Arriva Croydon and North Surrey operations merge with Arriva London South. This brought with it six additional 811Ds numbered MD430/1/4/5/6/8. They carried registration marks L430/1/4/5/6CPJ and P438HKN. They continued to operate from Beddington Farm garage, close to Croydon.

Metroline

Metroline was privatised on 7 October 1994. At this time, a number of Optare StarRider bodied 811Ds were taken into stock by the new company. These were numbered SR7/8, 54/5/7-9, 61/7/8, 81-5/7-90/2-6/8, 100/1/3/4, all being allocated to Edgware. SR7 quickly lost standard red livery in favour of Metroline Travel livery, this being done in October. A year later, in October 1995, SR8 was painted red with a thick white band and was allocated to Cricklewood. It soon gained an all-over advertisement for Safeway supermarkets, being used on a special service. In October 1995 SR67, 81, 84 and 90 were also repainted into a special livery for North London Railways, providing a rail replacement service between Camden Road and Willesden Junction. The quartet operated the service from Cricklewood.

The introduction of both step-entrance and low-floor Dennis Darts began to lead to the demise of the SR-class. The majority of Metroline's SRs had left London by the end of 1996, most being sold to Fleetmaster of Horsham.

Metroline painted four Optare StarRiders in a livery for the North London Railways in October 1995. SR90 (G90KUB) is seen departing Willesden Junction station on the special rail replacement service. *Mike Harris*

London Northern/Metroline

London Northern was privatised on 26 October 1994 and took SR108-118/20/1 into stock at this time. They were being used from Potters Bar on a couple of midibus routes in the Barnet area. They were withdrawn and sold en masse during April 1998 to Holts of Bolton.

London Northern also took stock of MW18 to MW37, all of which were allocated to Potters Bar. They passed to Metroline in August 1998. The first withdrawals of the type came in October 1998, the last of the type leaving London in April 2000.

London Northern purchased a solitary Marshall bodied 811D midibus for use on Potters Bar local service PB1. MMS269 (N161YEG) was delivered to the company in June 1996. It passed to Metroline in August 1998, retaining its original fleet number. It continued operating with Metroline until July 2005 when it was replaced by an Optare Solo.

Metrobus

As mentioned above, two former London Central SRs were acquired by Metrobus in 1997 (SR31 and SR41). In addition to these, four were acquired from East Surrey Buses, these carrying registration marks E318SYG, F670NPG, F70RPL and G301CPL. These remained operating with Metrobus until May 2000, when the last of them were sold by the company.

MERCEDES-BENZ 709D

Like the 811D, the Mercedes-Benz 709D was also part of the second-generation commercial vehicle chassis introduced by Mercedes-Benz in 1986. Unlike the 811D, fewer examples were operated by bus operators in the Greater London area.

London Buses Limited

In November 1988 the first Mercedes-Benz 709D midibuses arrived in London, these being bodied by Reeve Burgess. These vehicles took up rolling stock numbers MT1 to MT4 and were registered F391-4DHL. They were joined by MT5 (F395DHL) in January 1989. The quintet was operated on behalf of the London Borough of Ealing, operating new service E5 which linked Greenford Broadway with the Havelock Estate. MT1-5 were fitted with wide doors at the rear of the vehicle, along with a wheelchair lift, making the E5 a fully-wheelchair accessible service. A livery of red, with a white band edged with green, complete with Southall Shuttle logos, was worn by the batch. They also featured both London Buses and London Borough of Ealing logos. Operating from Hanwell, MT1-5 could also be found operating on mobility services in the Greenford and Ealing areas.

MT1 (F391DHL) represents the small batch of Reeve Burgess bodied Mercedes-Benz 709Ds allocated to Hanwell for use on the E5. The route was branded as the Southall Shuttle and gained a cream band with branding as seen above. *Ian Armstrong Collection*

Because of the success of the Southall Shuttle E5 service, an order was placed for two additional Mercedes-Benz 709Ds. Ford Transits were used to fill in until the new vehicles arrived. They did so in August 1989, numbered MT7 and MT8 (G537/8GBD), both being allocated to Hanwell for Mobility Routes. Like MT1-5, the pair featured rear doors and a wheelchair lift. Two years later, they were transferred to Uxbridge for use on Mobility routes. July 1991 saw MT5 and MT8 gain Mobility Bus livery, with MT7 following suit in August.

MT1 to MT5 transferred from Hanwell to the newly established Greenford garage in March 1993, the new site being shared with the London Borough of Ealing. They remained on the E5 until early 1994, at which time they were replaced by MA-class Mercedes-Benz 811Ds. After this, MT1-5 were shared between Victoria Basement, the Battersea midibus base, Stockwell and Catford for further use, mainly on Mobility services.

Centrewest/First London

At the time of privatisation, 2 September 1994, MT7 and MT8 passed to Centrewest, retaining their former London Buses fleet numbers. They continued to operate from Uxbridge. MT7 continued operating under Centrewest and later First London ownership until withdrawal in February 1997. MT8 lasted a little longer, passing to First Mainline in July 2000. It was reacquired by First London in July 2003. By this time, it had been renumbered 50177 in the First South Yorkshire fleet. Two additional 709Ds arrived in July 2006, also from First South Yorkshire. Numbered 50184 and 50186 (N117/9DWE), they were used as driver trainers from Westbourne Park.

Stagecoach London

Stagecoach took stock of MT4 (F394DHL) on 6 September 1994. It was allocated at Selkent's Orpington garage and used on mobility routes. It remained in use with Stagecoach London until May 2000 when it was sold.

London General/Go Ahead London

London General was another of the former London Buses operations to take stock of the 709D at the time of privatisation. From 2 November 1994 MT1-3, 5 passed to London General, operating from the Battersea Bridge midibus base. The first three remained with London General until they were withdrawn in 1996 or 1997. MT5 stayed a little longer, being sold in March 2000.

Epsom Buses

Epsom Buses was formed from the long-established Epsom Coaches. They purchased their first Mercedes-Benz midibus in 1986. In 1988 they purchased a batch of six 709Ds, four carrying Reeve Burgess Beaver bodies, the other two being bodied by Robin Hood. Wearing the maroon and cream livery associated with the company, they were put to use on commercial services 2 and 3, as well as operating Surrey County Council tendered services 516, 551 and 570, based on the Epsom area.

Those bodied by Reeve Burgess were registered E204/5YGC, E206BLN and F207DGT. The first pair arrived in March 1988, shortly followed by E206BLN. The final one arrived in August. The pair carrying Robin Hood bodies also arrived in August, being registered F208/9GGH. Those bodied by Reeve Burgess were operated by the company until December 2000, the Robin Hood saloons departing the fleet in 2001 and 1999 respectively.

Metrobus/Kentish Bus

Metrobus operated a fleet of eight Reeve Burgess bodied Mercedes-Benz 709Ds in the Gravesend area, being used on two services in competition with Kentish Bus. Two routes were established in the area, the A (Northfleet Plough–Gravesend–Denton–Valley Drive–Hever Court Road) and B (Painters Ash–Gravesend–Denton–Valley Driver–Hever Court Road). Commencing in August 1988, they were operated from the Green Street Green garage. The vehicles used on the route took rolling stock numbers 121 to 128 (F121-8TRU), all arriving in August. These wore a blue and yellow livery and were branded as Mini-Metro. However, by 1 January 1990 the routes and vehicles had passed to Kentish Bus.

In March 1991, four of the batch (123/5/6/8) returned to Metrobus for use on new route 351 (Bromley North–Penge). These did not last long on the route, being replaced by a batch of short Dennis Darts. Six of the eight were sold on to Luton & District for further use, lasting with them until the spring of 2000.

Beckenham High Street finds Metrobus 709D F126TRU, seen on its way to Penge on route 351. *Mike Harris*

Eastern National Citybus/Thamesway

Eastern National was one of the first non-red operators to win an LRT contract, taking on the W9 (Enfield–Muswell Hill Broadway) in 1985. This route had been one of the first to be operated by minibuses, using Ford Transits, being upgraded later to the BS-class Bristol LS. Eastern National had originally employed Bedford YMQs on the route. A fleet of sixteen Reeve Burgess bodied Mercedes-Benz 709D midibuses were purchased to upgrade the fleet on the route. These took stock numbers 0245 to 0260 and carried registration marks F245/6MVW, F247-52NJN and F253-60RHK. 245 and 246 arrived in August 1988, followed by 247 to 250 in November. 251 and 252 were delivered to the company in December. 253-6 and 260 entered the Eastern National fleet in February 1989, with 257 to 259 completing the batch in March.

Eastern National won the contract for the 379 (Chingford–Yardley Lane) from Grey-Green in March 1989, the new operator branding it the Enfield Hoppa. They were also successful in winning new routes W13 (Leytonstone–Woodford Wells) and W14 (Leyton–Woodford Bridge). 0245-0260 soon moved onto these routes.

Eastern National was acquired by the Badgerline Group in April 1990, and in July the London, Hornchurch and Southend garages were re-branded as Thamesway. Under this new operation, they won the contract for route 362 (Chadwell Heath–Barkingside), this starting on 1 December 1990. Six Reeve Burgess Beaver bodied 709Ds were purchased, arriving in November. Allocated to Brentwood, these midibuses took stock numbers 0301-0306 (H301-6LPU).

Route 193 (Oldchurch Hospital–Romford–Country Park Estate) was the next and final route to gain a fleet of Mercedes-Benz 709Ds. 0388 to 0395 (H388-95MAR) were purchased to replace the fleet of Mercedes-Benz L608Ds that had been used on the route. These put in an appearance in August 1991.

0252 (F252NJN) was taken into stock by Eastern National in 1988, passing to Thamesway in 1990. It was part of a batch of sixteen Mercedes-Benz 709Ds. It is seen wearing Thamesway livery whilst operating the 389 to Barnet. *Ian Armstrong Collection*

0256 (F256RHK) was another of the sixteen strong fleet of 709Ds taken into stock in 1988. It is seen wearing a simplified version of the Thamesway livery. *Ian Armstrong Collection*

0306 (H306LPU) was delivered to Thamesway in 1990 primarily for the 362. However, it is photographed on layover at Chingford Station whilst operating the 379. *Ian Armstrong Collection*

London Buslines

London Buslines won the contract for the C4 Chelsea Harbour Hoppa service which linked the site with Putney Pier. London Buslines was due to start operating the route in June 1990, but took it on two months early. Four Reeve Burgess bodied 709Ds were purchased for the route, along with use on the 518 on Sundays. These were numbered 644 to 647 (G644-7YVS). To compensate for the early start, four Mercedes-Benz 609Ds were used temporarily on the route, these being registered E459/60/8/71CGM, loaned from the Bee Line. The quartet remained operating with London Buslines for seven years before passing to First Eastern Counties in 1997.

County Bus

By October 1989, County Bus and Coach had won the contract for route 505 between Harlow and Walthamstow. Four Mercedes-Benz 709Ds were purchased for the route. These took up rolling stock numbers 914/5 and 918/9 (G914/5/8/9UPP) and were allocated to Harlow for the service.

In September 1990, five additional Reeve Burgess Beaver bodied 709Ds were acquired from Sovereign Bus and Coach. 901, 912-5 (G901/12-5UPP) were allocated to Grays to help fill in gaps on newly won LRT contracts 256 (Harold Hill–Hornchurch) and 346 (Upminster Station–Upminster Park Estate). This was a short-term arrangement, and by January 1991 these five midibuses had moved back to Sovereign.

Four additional 709Ds arrived in November 1991 registered J933-6WHJ. They took rolling stock numbers MB933-6 and were put to use on route W14, won from Thamesway. They were joined by MB937/8 (J937/8WHJ) in May 1992. All were allocated to Debden, an outstation of Harlow, and wore the Lea Valley name.

Sovereign

Sovereign originally took stock of twenty-one 709Ds in 1989 for the Hertfordshire operation, with some of these going on loan to County Bus, as mentioned above. The company had been successful in winning four LRT tenders in the Harrow area of North London which started in the autumn of 1990. Two of the original 709Ds, G908/9UPP, moved to the new Harrow base prior to this to act as driver trainers for the new fleet on order.

They acquired the old Venture base and set up a subsidiary company. Two of these, the H11 (Northwood Park–Northwick Park Hospital) and H13 (Northwood Hills–Ruislip Lido), commenced operation in December. For these two services, a fleet of twelve Mercedes-Benz 709Ds were purchased and used on these services. Arriving in November, these vehicles took up registration marks H920-3/5-7/9-31FGS. Sovereign (Harrow) was successful in winning the contract for the H17 from R&I Tours in February 1991, with members of this batch seeing service on the route. The batch gained rolling stock numbers matching the numbers in their registration marks – 920-3/5-7/9-31 – in 1993. The 709Ds were replaced by low-floor Plaxton Pointer bodied Dennis Dart SLFs in 1999, the Mercedes minibuses being sold after this time.

Route H13 was one of two routes in the Harrow area to benefit from a fleet of 709Ds. H923FGS is seen loading before departing for Northwood Hills. *Ian Armstrong Collection*

Sister vehicle H925FGS is photographed on the other route, the H11. It is seen on layover at Harrow bus station. *Ian Armstrong Collection*

Armchair

Brentford based Armchair purchased a solitary Mercedes-Benz 709D, bodied by Reeve Burgess. It was delivered to Armchair in October 1989 registered G94VMM. The company used it on the recently won Surrey County Council route 564, won from London & Country. The vehicle lasted with the company until 1998.

Transcity

Transcity of Sidcup operated a solitary Carlyle bodied 709D midibus in January 1991. Registered H149NOJ, it was supported by the small fleet of Talbot Pullmans being used by Transcity on the B15.

Capital Coaches/Capital Logistics/ Tellings-Golden Miller

Heathrow-based coach operator Capital Coaches won their first LRT contract in 1993. This was the Hounslow Hoppa H26 service linking Hatton Cross with Sparrow Farm Estate. Three 709Ds arrived in November 1993 registered L204-6ULX. Like the MT-class operating with London Buses, this trio also featured rear doors and a wheelchair lift. A livery of white with green relief was applied to these vehicles, complete with Hounslow Hoppa names.

Two additional 709Ds arrived in 1997 registered P255/6MLE, gaining fleet numbers CS4 and CS5. They also featured rear doors and a tail lift and carried the new Plaxton Beaver body style. CS4 arrived in January, whilst CS5 put in an appearance during April. By this time, Capital Coaches had been renamed Capital Logistics.

In June 1999, the company was acquired by Tellings-Golden Miller. Under the new owner, rolling stock numbers 4-6 and 55/6 were allocated to them. Tellings-Golden Miller itself was formed in 1985 when Byfleet-based Tellings Coaches merged with Golden Miller of Feltham. At the time this took place, an Onyx bodied 709D was already in operation, this carrying registration mark F71SJX.

Prior to the acquisition of Capital Logistics, Tellings-Golden Miller were operating six Mercedes-Benz 709Ds, all carrying Plaxton Beaver bodies. Three (M70, 80, 90TGM) were taken into stock in April 1995 for use on route S3 (Worcester Park–Belmont Station). They were supported by coach-seated M60TGM. The fifth 709D was registered N70TGM, and arrived in January 1996 for use on the K3. The final 709D to enter the fleet did so in June 1997 registered P70TGM. These were later numbered 7-9, 17, 27 by the company.

Epsom Buses won the contract for the S3 in March 2000, with four 709Ds (M70, 80, 90TGM, N70TGM) placed on loan for a month. They returned to Tellings-Golden Miller in April 2000 for further use on Surrey routes 426 and 441 from Byfleet.

27 (P70TGM) was stolen in May 2003, and was subsequently burnt out. The introduction of low-floor Dennis Dart SLFs meant that others moved on to MK Metro in Milton Keynes for further use. 56 (P256MLE) was the last of the type to operate with the company, transferring to Travel London in June 2005. It became the last step-entrance vehicle to operate a TfL service, being withdrawn in December 2005 after route H21 was withdrawn.

P255MLE, a Plaxton Beaver bodied Mercedes-Benz 709D, was new to Capital Logistics of West Drayton in January 1997. It passed to Tellings-Golden Miller along with the Capital Logistics business in 1999. It is seen wearing the livery of its new owners whilst loading at Staines bus station. *Ian Armstrong Collection*

M90TGM was new to Tellings-Golden Miller in April 1995 for the S3 in the Sutton area. It is seen wearing the smart livery of the company whilst heading towards Sutton Hospital. *Matthew Wharmby*

Docklands Buses

Docklands Buses of Silvertown never purchased any Mercedes-Benz 709D minibuses. However, one was operated by them in July 1995. It was at this time that sister company Thames Transit, Oxford, loaned a 709D numbered 322 (F322EJO) for use on routes 287 and 366.

First Capital

First Capital assumed control of Thamesway's garage at Ponders End in August 1998. The fleet of 709Ds that were in use on LRT contracts from this garage were taken into stock by First Capital. Former 0245/6, 0251/3-8 (F245/6MVW, F251NJN, F253-8RHK) were renumbered 565/9, 561/3, 570, 562/6/7/8 by their new owner. Also, 301-6 (H301-6LPU) became 581 to 586, and 388-95 took new fleet numbers 588 to 595. They remained operational until being sold between July 2000 and March 2001.

Crystals

Crystals of Dartford also took stock of a solitary Mercedes-Benz 709D, bodied by Crystals. It was taken into stock by the company in February 1997 registered P347HKU. It was put to use on Mobility routes 931-7 and 970-3. It passed to Tellings-Golden Miller in August 2003.

CVE OMNI

CVE was built near Darlington from 1988 but being introduced later than other minibus models, it did not have much success with normal bus operators. It did, however, have more success in the welfare sector. Very few of the type were operated in London, with only a handful being operated by London Buses Limited and later Westlink.

London Buses Limited

The first CVEs arrived with the Westlink subsidiary in March 1989. Numbered CV1 to CV3, they were registered F265-7WDC. Allocated to Hounslow Heath, they were put to use on the H20 (Hounslow Civic Centre–Ivybridge Estate). CV1 and CV3 wore an all-white livery, with CV2 operating in all-red. Owned by the London Borough of Hounslow, these vehicles seated twenty people, and could carry up to two wheelchairs, the seating capacity being reduced if two were carried.

Three CVE Omnis were loaned between May and September 1989. F369TVN arrived in May, being painted into red. F976WEF soon followed, operating in an all-white livery, relieved by a light blue skirt. F295WPY was the final loaned vehicle, arriving in September. This wore a white-based livery, with a green skirt.

A fourth CVE Omni was purchased by London Buses, arriving in November. CV4 (F268WDC) was allocated to London General's Victoria Basement garage. It was put to use on Carelink services, wearing a dedicated livery. Unlike CV1-3, the wheelchair lift on CV4 was located at the front of the vehicle. CV4 transferred to Harrow Weald garage in May 1991 which was in need of a wheelchair accessible minibus at this time. It gained a repaint into red before transferring.

A couple of years passed before the next CVEs arrived in the capital. Westlink took stock of CV5 and CV6 (G195/6CHN), acquired from C&M Coaches, Aintree, Merseyside. They were allocated to Hounslow Heath for use on routes R61 (Richmond–Queen Mary's Hospital) and R62 (Teddington–West Middlesex Hospital). They were soon re-registered A2/3LBR. A month later, CV7 was taken into stock, this carrying registration mark A4LBR.

The Department of Transport loaned K264BGM to Westlink in May 1993. It operated from Hounslow Heath for several months before passing to Capital Coaches in late 1993.

CV1-3/5-7 were transferred to Westlink when the company was purchased by the National Express Group in January 1994. They continued operating and were acquired by London United on 15 September 1995, when this company purchased the Westlink operation. They continued in service until March 1996 when they were sold.

CVE Omni CV5 (A2LBR) represents the small batch of the type to operate with London Buses in West London. It is seen on route R62 to Teddington, wearing Hoppa branding. *Ian Armstrong Collection*

K264BGM was loaned to Westlink from the Ministry of Transport over the summer months of 1993. It is seen attending a bus rally at North Weald, Essex. *Jeff Lloyd*

RENAULT S75

The Renault S75 was one of several minibuses to have evolved from the Dodge 50 chassis. The S75 was a 33-seater 7.5-tonne minibus. A sizeable batch were operated by London Buses on routes in west London.

The RW-class were predominantly used in West London, mainly in the Greenford and Ealing areas. RW1 (HDZ5401) is seen on layover in Greenford showing off the Ealing Buses names applied to these vehicles. *Ian Armstrong Collection*

London Buses Limited

Ninety Wright bodied Renault S75 midibuses were purchased by London Buses Limited during 1990, all being allocated to Centrewest for use in West London. Fourteen of these were allocated to route 282 (Mount Vernon Hospital–Ealing Hospital), the other seventy-six being used on the midibus scheme in the Ealing area, all originally being allocated to Hanwell garage.

The first arrived in February 1990, taking stock numbers RW1, 3-19. The batch gained registration marks in the Northern Ireland system; these being HDZ5401/3-19. RW2, 20-2 (HDZ5402 etc) followed in March. RW1-14 were the fourteen RWs intended

for route 282, with others also being used as and when needed, for this they gained Hoppa branding. The RWs took over route 282 from 3 March 1990, displacing MCW Metrobuses from the route. RW19 and RW21 were loaned to East London at Bow from where they were used on route 276, covering for a shortfall in RB-class Renault S50 midibuses.

Deliveries continued in April when RW23 and RW24 (HDZ5423/4) arrived. These were followed by RW25-48 (HDZ5428-48) in May. Numbers were boosted by the arrival of RW49-60 (HDZ5449-60) in June and RW61-72 in July.

Three of the new deliveries, RW52 to RW54, were loaned to Selkent in July 1990, being used on driver training duties from Catford. They moved west in time for service changes in Ealing.

The outstanding members of the batch arrived in September, numbered RW73-90 (HDZ5473-90). At this time, RW75 and RW76 were placed on short-term loan to Selkent, this time being allocated to Plumstead.

A number of the RW-class operated from Acton Tramshed, this being an outstation of Hanwell at the time, and as such it did not have a set allocation. However, this changed in September 1990 when RW26-48 were officially transferred on a permanent basis. RW15-90 carried Ealing Buses fleet names. Little of interest took place with this batch during their London service.

RW13 was severely damaged by fire in May 1994, and was subsequently withdrawn, being dismantled at Acton.

RW24 (HDZ5424) was another Renault S75 midibus, seen on route 195 to Ealing Hospital. *Ian Armstrong Collection*

Route 282 was the first route to gain a fleet of RW-class Renaults. RW57 (HDZ5457) is seen operating the route, heading towards Mount Vernon Hospital. *Ian Armstrong Collection*

The Ealing Buses fleet names can again be seen clearly on RW68 (HDZ5468) which is seen making its way to Ealing Broadway on the E8. *Ian Armstrong Collection*

Ealing Broadway finds RW72 (HDZ5472) on the E9 and RW22 (HDZ5422) on the E7. *Ian Armstrong Collection*

RW89 (HDZ5489) was the penultimate member of the ninety-strong batch of Renault S75s. It is seen operating route E4. *Ian Armstrong Collection*

Centrewest/First London

RW1-11, 14-90 passed to Centrewest upon privatisation of this subsidiary on 2 September 1994, continuing to operate in the Ealing area. Again, little of interest happened to the batch under the ownership of Centrewest. RW28 was re-registered in July 1995 from HDZ5428 to G397CLD after it was withdrawn. Withdrawal of the remaining RWs began in May 1996 when RW3, 5, 9, 10/3, 20-2/5 moved to sister company Bee Line, Bracknell. RW1, 2, 6, 16/8/9, 27/9, 30 followed in June. By May 1997, the type had been withdrawn, with the remaining members of the fleet passing to either Bee Line or Leicester Citybus.

RENAULT S50

Like the Renault S75, the Renault S50 evolved out of the Dodge S50 minibus model. A small number of the type were operated by London Buses during the 1990s.

London Buses Limited

Thirty-five Renault S50 midibuses were operated by London Buses Limited between 1990 and 1994, all of which were allocated to the East London division at Bow. It was from this garage that they were put to use on the 100 (Shadwell–Liverpool Street), 276 (Stoke Newington–North Woolwich Ferry) and S2 (Stratford–Clapton), with a Sunday extension to the Lea Valley Ice Centre.

The first members of the batch arrived in January 1990. Numbered RB1-5, 7/8, 21 (G871-5/7/8, 891WML), they were used as type trainers. RB6, 9 and 12 (G876/9, 882WML) followed in February, also being used at Bow as type trainers. Delivery of the first twenty-five RB-class midibuses was complete in March 1990 when RB10/1, 13-20/2-5 (G880/1/3-90/2-5WML) arrived. The last four (RB22-25) featured rear luggage boots.

A delay in the delivery of members of this batch led to the loan of some RW-class Renault S75 saloons from Hanwell, along with a handful of Leyland Nationals from West Ham. The RBs were used on the routes mentioned above, working alongside SR-class Mercedes-Benz 811Ds.

Deliveries recommenced in September 1990. It was at this time that RB26 and RB27 were taken into stock at Bow. RB28 to RB33 followed in October. Registration marks H126-33AML were allocated to these vehicles. This new batch displaced SR-class 811Ds to London Central who allocated them to Camberwell. RB1-33 carried Reeve Burgess Beaver bodywork.

In the closing months of 1991, two Plaxton Beaver bodied Renault S50s were leased by London Buses. Registered J134HME and J235LLK, the pair slotted into the numbering sequence as RB34 and RB35. RB34 arrived in November, whilst RB35 put in an appearance in December. These operated for a short time in London, with RB34 returning off lease in November 1992, RB35 following in March 1993.

RB35 had been placed on loan with London Buslines in May 1992, the company using it on routes 201 and 203. RB13 and RB16 were placed on loan with Kentish Bus in March 1993.

A number of the type were sold prior to the privatisation of London Buses Limited, these leaving London in the summer of 1994. However, in September, RB5/6, 10, 19-23 were re-allocated to Centrewest who used them from Hanwell in the Greenford and Ealing areas. These were operated by Centrewest until March 1995 when they were sold. One other, RB12, survived into privatisation, being owned very briefly by Stagecoach London. The original thirty-three were all sold to the Yorkshire Traction Group, seeing further service with either Yorkshire Traction, Lincolnshire Road Car or Strathtay Scottish.

The RB-class were allocated to the East London division of London Buses for three routes. One of these was the 100. It is on this route that we find RB9 (G879WML). *Ian Armstrong Collection*

The S2 was another of the three routes operated by the RB-class. RB18 (G888WML) is seen heading to Lea Valley Stores on the route, carrying the Hoppa branding. *Ian Armstrong Collection*

TALBOT PULLMAN

The Talbot Pullman was based on the Italian Express van, this being a joint venture between Fiat and Peugeot. The small nature of the vehicle meant that the Pullman was ideal for dial-a-ride schemes and small bus work. Rights to the Pullman model were sold to Talbot-Pullman in 1990, with the model continuing to be built. The Pullman Express model was later replaced by the Peugeot Boxer minibus.

Transcity, Sidcup

Transcity's G146TGX is captured by the camera whilst on layover at Welling Corner. *Mike Harris*

Sidcup-based Transcity purchased five Talbot Pullman minibuses for use on LRT route B15 (Welling–Bexleyheath–Joydens Wood), the route starting in January 1991. The quintet was registered F814AVC, G133AHP, G213/4AHP and G640BHP. They wore a green livery, with the exception of G214AHP which gained an all-over advertisement for RTM, Radio Thamesmead. The Transcity operation passed to Kentish Bus ownership on 29 October 1993.

Kentish Bus

In addition to the Talbot Pullmans mentioned above, Kentish Bus took stock of a small batch of fifteen Talbot Pullman saloons for operation just outside the London area, these being allocated to Dunton Green. The first six arrived in December 1989. Numbered 872/4/6, 881/2/5, they were registered G872SKE etc. The other members of the batch did not arrive until the first part of 1990. 870/1/5/9, 880/3/4 (G870SKE etc) put in an appearance in January; followed by 873 and 878 (G873/8SKE) in February. These vehicles were given Kentish Hopper fleet names. After the Talbots arrived, MetroRiders transferred from Dunton Green to Dartford and Northfleet garages.

Several Talbot Pullmans were loaned to Kentish Bus in 1989, these being originally allocated to Northfleet before joining the others at Dunton Green. The first arrived in April registered F481SDU. This vehicle was loaned again, along with sister F482SDU, in July. F516OKV, F914KRJ and F760TVC followed in August. The first two were returned off loan in November, whilst the latter vehicle remained with the company until February 1990. F914KRJ reappeared with Kentish Bus for a few days in January 1990, this again being used at Dunton Green.

Another Talbot Pullman was acquired by Kentish Bus in November 1993. Registered F393DOA, it was sourced from Pathfinder Tours of Collingham. Allocated to Dartford, the bus took up rolling stock number 836.

884 (G884SKE) is photographed on layover at West Croydon before setting off on its journey to Sevenoaks on route 23.
Bill Young

F393DOA was acquired by Kentish Bus from Pathfinder. It is seen wearing the green and yellow livery adopted by Kentish Bus.
Glyn Matthews

RENAULT S56

The Renault S56 was a third variant to be based on the Dodge S50 minibus. The S56 was smaller than the S75 model mentioned earlier in this book. Weighing 6-tonne, the S56 was able to seat twenty-five passengers.

London Country South West/London & Country

Seven Northern Counties bodied Renault-Dodge S56 minibuses arrived with London Country (South West) in October 1989. These were numbered 103 to 109 by the company, and they carried registration marks G103-9DPB. It took a while for these buses to gain rolling stock numbers, these not being applied until June 1990. Whilst Dorking took stock of 103 and 104, the others were originally allocated to Addlestone. Initially being used on local services in the area, they were put to use on two London routes, the K5 (Kingston–New Malden) and K6 (Ham–Kingston Vale), Robin Hood Estate). London & Country took up these routes from 8 May 1993. Operating for a couple of years, new rolling stock took over in the mid-1990s.

Seven Northern Counties bodied Renault-Dodge S56 midibuses were acquired in October 1989. In May 1993 they took up service on the K5 and K6 in the Kingston area. 105 (G105DPB) is seen on its way to Kingston Vale whilst operating the K6. *Ian Armstrong Collection*

Similar 107 (G107DPB) is seen on loading at Fairfield bus station in Kingston before continuing its journey to New Malden. *Ian Armstrong Collection*

London Buslines

London Buslines purchased three Plaxton bodied Renault S56 minibuses for use on Mobility Bus routes in the Brent, Harrow and Ealing areas, these being numbered 980 to 982. Registered K651-3DBL, these vehicles wore London Buslines livery, relieved by a red band on the lower bodywork. The trio put in an appearance in December 1992.

London Buslines 651 (K651DBL) was one of three Renault S56 minibuses purchased by the company for mobility work in West London. It was photographed whilst on layover at Park Royal Asda. *Mike Harris*

VOLVO B6

The B6 was Volvo's attempt to compete with the Dennis Dart. Whilst the type proved to be popular outside London, the Dart was the chosen model for the majority of London's single-deck needs of the early 1990s. However, a number of Volvo B6 saloons were taken into stock by various London operators, carrying either the Alexander Dash, Northern Counties or Plaxton Pointer bodywork.

Capital Citybus

Capital Citybus became the first operator of the Volvo B6, taking sixteen into stock. The first ten arrived in January and February 1994, carrying Alexander Dash bodywork. Numbered 671 to 680 (L671-80RMD), they displaced older, smaller midibuses on the 236 (Finsbury Park–Hackney Wick). They wore the distinctive yellow livery of Capital Citybus, retaining this livery until ownership passed to First Group. They eventually succumbed to the red and yellow livery under the 80 per cent red rule introduced by Transport for London. The fleet of Volvo B6s underwent modification work leading to the loan of M262KWK from Volvo, Warwick, this operating on the 236 from Dagenham.

Ten Alexander
Dash bodied Volvo B6 saloons were purchased by Capital Citybus in 1994 to operate the 236. The first of these, 671 (L671RMD), is seen about to enter Finsbury Park Station wearing the smart yellow Capital Citybus livery.
Jeff Lloyd

These were joined by three Northern Counties Paladin bodied B6 saloons numbered 681 to 683. Registration marks L281RML, L888TJC and L888AMY were allocated to the trio. Arriving in April 1994, they were put to use on the D5 (Mile End–Crossharbour Asda).

In April 1996, another three Northern Counties bodied Volvo B6 saloons were taken into stock, this time being acquired from Flightpark of Gatwick Airport. These continued the fleet numbering sequence as 684 to 686 (L4-6GML). They were put to use on route 396 between Ilford Broadway and Goodmayes. These remained with Capital Citybus until October 1999, at which time they passed to First Leicester (694) or First Northampton (695/6).

Finsbury Park also provides the location of this photograph of 679 (L679RMD), seen keeping company with an Arriva London Routemaster on route 19. By the time this photograph had been taken, the livery worn by Capital Citybus vehicles had been slightly modified. *Ian Armstrong Collection*

The first of three Northern Counties bodied Volvo B6s to be taken into stock by Capital Citybus in April 1994, 681 (L281RML), is seen passing Stagecoach East London's Leyton garage on its way to Chingford Station. *Jeff Lloyd*

By October 2000, 671-8 had been displaced from the 236 and W11 by low-floor Dart SLFs. After this time, six transferred to St Mary Cray for use on the seasonal Bromley Park & Ride service. The other two were transferred to Centrewest for use on the 295. By the end of 2000, the Alexander Dash bodied B6s departed London, passing to neighbouring First Essex.

683 (L888AMY) is seen heading towards Ilford Broadway whilst operating route 396. This was the last of the three B6s to enter the Capital Citybus fleet in April 1994. *Jeff Lloyd*

Two years after the first three Northern Counties bodied Volvo B6 saloons entered the Capital Citybus fleet, three more were taken into stock. 685 (L5GML) was the middle member of the batch which were acquired in April 1996 from Flightpark of Gatwick Airport. *Jeff Lloyd*

Kentish Bus/Londonlinks

Kentish Bus was successful in winning a number of London contracts in 1994, the majority of which were operated using Northern Counties bodied Dennis Darts. However, twelve 9.9m Northern Counties Paladin bodied B6s were operated on route 108 (Lewisham–Stratford). Registration marks L201-12YCU were allocated to these saloons along with fleet numbers 201 to 212. They wore the maroon and cream livery associated with Kentish Bus and were allocated to the company's Lewisham garage. The route was lost to Harris Bus in April 1997, after which time the B6s transferred to Londonlinks at Croydon. They were put to use on the 127 between Purley and Tooting Broadway. In June 1998 they transferred to Arriva Croydon & North Surrey, still operating from Beddington Farm. In 1999 the batch transferred to Arriva West Sussex for further use in the Crawley area.

Kentish Bus operated a small batch of Northern Counties bodied Volvo B6 saloons. Twelve examples arrived in 1994 for use on the 108. 206 (L206YCU) represents these vehicles as it heads to Lewisham on the 108 wearing the maroon and cream Kentish Bus livery. *Ian Armstrong Collection*

The twelve B6s that had originated with Kentish Bus moved to sister company Londonlinks in 1997. They were put to use on route 127 (Purley–Tooting Broadway) and were given branding for the service. 203 (L203YCU) is seen carrying this branding as it loads on its way to Purley. *Ian Armstrong Collection*

Sutton finds
Londonlinks Volvo B6 205 (L205YCU). It is seen shortly before reaching journey's end. *Ian Armstrong Collection*

London Buses Limited

A solitary Plaxton Pointer bodied Volvo B6 saloon was placed on loan for five days during June 1994. Registered L608WWK, it operated from North Street, Romford for the duration of its stay.

Stagecoach London

The final Volvo B6s to be taken into stock by a London operator arrived in 1995. A number of Alexander Dash bodied B6s were taken into stock by Stagecoach London and were allocated to the East London operation. All arrived during March 1995, and were all diverted from other Stagecoach operations. 1301 to 1310 (M741-6, 847, 748-50PRS) came from Stagecoach Ribble, having briefly been used in Morecambe. They wore the Stagecoach white and stripes corporate livery and were used on the 247 (Romford–Barkingside) and 499 (Romford, North Street–Romford, Parkside Hotel). 1311 (M846HDF) joined them, arriving from Stagecoach Cheltenham & Gloucester.

The final six were allocated to Leyton, used primarily as driver trainers, again wearing the Stagecoach white and stripe livery. Registration marks M453-8VHE were carried by 453 to 458. This small batch was taken into stock from Stagecoach East Midlands. Their arrival allowed for Leyland Titans to transfer from Leyton to Barking to convert route 238 back to double-deck operation. It also allowed DRL-class Darts to transfer between Romford and Barking.

1301-10 left London during April, passing back to Stagecoach Ribble. 453-8 and 1311 left London, doing so in May 1995, with 453-8 passing to Stagecoach Ribble.

Early 1995 saw a number of Alexander Dash bodied Volvo B6 saloons enter service with Stagecoach East London on a couple of services in East London. They had been diverted from other Stagecoach operations and were operated by the company in the provincial white with orange, red and blue stripes livery. This is shown by 1302 (M742PRS), an example new to Stagecoach Ribble. *Ian Armstrong Collection*

IVECO 59.12/MARSHALL

The Iveco 59.12 was a larger variant of the Iveco Dailybus minibus. The 59.12 was the heaviest of the Iveco minibuses, weighing 6 tonnes.

County Bus

County Bus was the only operator of the Iveco 59.12 midibus in the London area. Four Marshall bodied 59.12s were taken into stock by County Bus in June 1994. Numbered MBT713 to MBT716 (L713-6OVX), they were allocated to Edmonton garage. The company won the contracts for a number of Mobility routes from Capital Citybus. The quartet wore a red and cream livery for these services. County Bus was renamed Arriva East Herts & Essex in 1997. On 3 October 1998, Edmonton garage passed to the ownership of Arriva London, with MBT713-6 passing to the new owner for continued use.

MBT714 (L714OVX) was one of four Marshall bodied Iveco 59.12 minibuses purchased by County Bus & Coach for use on mobility services. It is seen passing through Stratford Broadway on its way to Walthamstow. *Mike Harris*

LDV CONVOY

The LDV Convoy was in the true sense a van-derived minibus, becoming popular with a number of local authorities and community transport operators around the United Kingdom.

Centrewest/First London

A large number of LDV Convoy minibuses were operated in London by a range of independent operators, along with community transport and local authorities. However, three 12-seater LDV Convoys were purchased by Centrewest for use on a contract for the London Borough of Richmond. Numbered LC1 to LC3, registration marks N921-3LUF were given to these vehicles. Arriving in October 1995, they were allocated to Westbourne Park for the duration of their stay. LC2 and LC3 were both written off by September 2003 following accidents. LC1 survived with Centrewest until May 2006, at which time it was sold.

MAN 11.220/MARSHALL

The MAN 11.220 chassis was introduced to London in 1996, and was of a similar length to the Volvo B6 introduced a couple of years before. It was another type that was not taken up in large numbers, with a modest batch operating in London between 1996 and 2005. The Marshall C31 was the chosen body style for those operated in the Capital, these measuring 10.0m.

R&I Buses/MTL London Northern

R&I Buses took stock of the MAN 11.220 chassis during 1996, these all carrying Marshall bodywork. The first arrived in April, taking rolling stock numbers MM254 to MM265. These were followed in June by MM266 to MM268. The batch took up registration marks N121-35XEG. All were allocated to North Acton, from where they were used on the 95 (Southall–Shepherds Bush Green). These operated for a very short

MTL London
Northern chose the Marshall bodied MAN 11.240 single-deck for its 1996 deliveries. MM272 (P472JEG) is seen loading at Edgware bus station before departing to Alperton on route 79. *Ian Armstrong Collection*

period of time with R&I, the vehicles and routes operated by this company passing to MTL London Northern in June. The new operator continued to use the type on the 95.

A further eight of the type were taken into stock by MTL London Northern in December 1996 (MM270-6/8) or January 1997 (MM277). Registered P470-8JEG, these were again allocated to North Acton, this time for use on the 79 (Edgware Station–Alperton).

MM254-278 all passed to Metroline in August 1998, retaining their former London Northern fleet numbers. They continued operating these routes from North Acton until September 2000 when the garage was closed, moving then to nearby Harlesden. The traditional red and blue skirt livery of Metroline was applied to the batch.

MM272 to MM275 transferred to the Commercial Services fleet based at Cricklewood in July 2001. In September, MM273 gained a dark blue livery for use on a contract for Tesco. The first nine MMs left London in September, with the remaining members of the fleet being withdrawn between May and November 2005.

August 1998 saw the fleet of Marshall bodied MAN 11.240 saloons pass from MTL London ownership to that of Metroline. MM271 (P471JEG) is photographed at Alperton Sainsbury's before heading to Edgware. *Ian Armstrong Collection*

OPTARE EXCEL

The Optare Excel was launched in October 1995, being the first low-floor vehicle offered by Optare. The Excel was available in a range of lengths measuring between 9.6m and 11.5m. Those used on London services were either the 9.6m or 10.7m variant, all of which are detailed below.

Thorpes

F.E. Thorpe of Wembley was the first user of the Optare Excel in London. Four 9.6m Excels, N100, 200, 300, 400FET, were purchased in June 1996 for use on the Stationlink services SL1 and SL2. These connected the main Central London railway termini with each other. These remained in use until July 2002 when they were sold. At this time, N100FET was re-registered N608JLY, and N300FET became N643JLY. The other two were exported.

The Stationlink services were increased in frequency in 2001, leading to another two Excels being purchased by Thorpes in July. Registered R845/6FWW, the pair originated with A1A of Birkenhead. They took up fleet numbers XL845 and XL846, and remained with the company until April 2004.

F.E. Thorpe operated two Stationlink routes linking the Central London rail termini. 2001 saw an increase in frequency, leading to two Optare Excels being sourced from A1A of Birkenhead. They joined four similar vehicles that had been operating the route since 1996. R846FWW is seen operating route SL2 at Marble Arch. *Ian Armstrong Collection*

Metrobus

Route 358 (Orpington–Bromley–Crystal Palace) was one of Metrobus' more successful routes. The increase in patronage on the route had seen the original batch of Dennis Darts, that had been introduced on the route in 1992, operating the routes until they were replaced by larger capacity Darts in 1993. However, by 1996 larger vehicles were again required for the service. For this, ten longer 10.7m Optare Excels were purchased by Metrobus for use on the route. P501-10OUG were taken into stock by the company in July (P501) and August 1996 (P502-10). Wearing the distinctive yellow and blue livery associated with Metrobus, they operated from the company's garage at Green Street Green. They later took up rolling stock numbers 501 to 510.

A solitary Optare Excel 2 model was placed on long-term loan for evaluation against the original model, this being used on route 353. Registered V511KMY, it slotted in the Metrobus fleet as 511, arriving in December 1999.

The withdrawal of Arriva Southern Counties from Crawley in March 2001 meant that the original ten Excels moved to the Sussex town for use on town services. These left the Metrobus fleet in July 2002, passing to the Birmingham Coach Company of Tividale.

P503OUG represents the original ten Optare Excel saloons purchased by Metrobus in 1996 for route 358. It is seen wearing the blue and yellow livery synonymous with Metrobus. *Ian Armstrong Collection*`

London United

A small batch of Optare Excels were operated by the Westlink operation of London United, arriving in 1997. Prior to their arrival, an Excel was loaned between March and June 1997. Registered P446SWX, it was allocated to Kingston.

XL1-4/6/7 (P151BUG etc) arrived at Westlink's Kingston garage in June 1997, displacing a batch of Optare Vecta bodied MAN saloons from route 371 (Richmond–Kingston). Measuring 10.0m, they wore the red, with white roof and grey skirt livery, complete with route branding and Westlink fleet names. They remained at Kingston until that garage closed in November 2001, at which time they moved to the new Tolworth garage. In January 2002 their place on the 371 was taken by new Plaxton Pointer bodied Dennis Dart SLF saloons. The Excels then moved to Hounslow for use on the 110 (Twickenham–Hounslow). The end came in May 2003 when Dart SLFs displaced the Excels at Hounslow.

Six Optare Excels were taken into stock by London United in the first half of 1997 for use on the 371 between Richmond and Kingston. The first of these, XL1 (P151BUG), is seen heading towards the latter destination. *Ian Armstrong Collection*

Harris Bus/East Thames Buses

Harris Bus updated its fleet in 1996, introducing a new smart livery of pale green and blue. Four Optare Excels were purchased in October 1996 for routes 383, 384 and 385 (Lakeside–Tilbury–Chadwell St Mary). Registration marks P320-3KAR were allocated to the batch, these taking up fleet numbers 320 to 323. The vehicles gained route branding, along with 'Thurrock Link' fleet names.

Optare Excel demonstrator P446SWX was operated by Harris Bus for a short period of time during 1998, being put to use on the Thurrock service.

The company won its first London bus contract in 1997, the first being school route 661, and later the 108 (Stratford–Lewisham), this commencing operation in April 1997. A fleet of eleven 10.7m Excels were purchased for the route, following on from the Thurrock batch as 324 to 334 (P324-332NHJ, P333HBC, P334NHJ), being delivered to the company in April. They wore a similar livery to 320-3, gaining route branding and 'Lewisham Link' fleet names. The route was operated from a newly established outstation in the Crayford area.

Another single-deck London contract was won by Harris Bus in 1998, this being the 132 (Eltham Station–Bexleyheath). For this, eight Excels were purchased. Again, wearing the pale green and blue livery, they were given route branding and 'Eltham Link' fleet names. Fleet numbers 373-80 were allocated to these vehicles, along with registration marks R373-80DJN. 373 and 374 arrived in December 1997, the rest following in January 1998.

Harris Bus ran into financial trouble in 1999, with the operations passing to London Buses Limited in December 1999. From this date, 324-34 and 373-80 were taken on by the new company, trading as East Thames Buses. The Excels gained the 'XL' classification code in front of their former Harris Bus numbers. Over the course of 2000, the bright livery of Harris Bus was replaced by an all-red livery, relieved only by East Thames Buses fleet names.

Harris Bus purchased eleven Optare Excel saloons for the 108 in 1997. 328 (P328NHJ) represents the batch. The route branding applied to the fleet can be seen on 328 which is photographed having reached the Lewisham end of the service. *Matthew Wharmby*

By July 2002 the Excels used on the 132 had been displaced by step-entrance Volvo Olympians, the Excels being confined to the 108. XL332 was the victim of a fire in Lewisham in November 2002, and was placed into store at Ash Grove at this time, along with six other Excels. In January 2003, XL328 and XL331 also caught fire, these also being withdrawn. The final Excels left London in December 2006, being sold for further service.

377 (R377DJN) was one of eight Optare Excels purchased by Harris Bus for use on the 132 in south-east London. The route was branded as the 'Eltham Link'. This is shown by 377 which is seen on layover at Eltham Station. *Matthew Wharmby*

375 (R375DJN) was new to Harris Bus, passing to East Thames Buses in 1999. It is seen at Romford station starting its journey to Leytonstone on route 66. *David Beddall*

702 (P702HMT) was the second of four Optare Excels taken into stock by Capital Citybus in November 1996. It is photographed operating route 396 to Ilford Broadway. *Ian Armstrong Collection*

Capital Citybus

Capital Citybus took stock of four Optare Excel saloons in November 1996. These were numbered 701 to 704 and carried registration marks P701-4HMT. Wearing the yellow Capital Citybus livery, they were put to use on the 396.

Capital Logistics/Tellings-Golden Miller/Travel London

Capital Logistics had primarily been involved in both coach and airport contracts based at Heathrow Airport. Their first London contract was won in August 1993, taking up service on the H26 using minibuses. A Sunday service on the H24 was added to their portfolio in March 1998, followed by the 726 (Heathrow Airport–Dartford) in April. Another contract was won, commencing in May 1998. The U3 (Heathrow Airport Central–Uxbridge) was won from Centrewest, and for this a batch of nine 10.0m Optare Excels were purchased. Registration marks R985-92EWU were carried by these vehicles, these arriving in April and May.

Tellings-Golden Miller purchased Capital Logistics in June 1999, with the U3 and its Excels passing to the new owner. They gained the white, yellow and blue livery of

their new owner during the latter part of 2000. Originally operating from the former Capital Logistics premises in West Drayton, Tellings-Golden Miller rented part of the Fulwell garage, moving all of its London operations to the new base, the Excels being reallocated there in April 2000.

In April 2001, the Excels were moved from the U3 to the 490. By this time, 987 had left the fleet. Another route change took place in June 2002, the Excels moving onto the 216 (Staines–Kingston), operating the route until it was lost in June 2003. After this time, they were placed into store. The acquisition of Crystals in the Orpington area meant that the Excels moved into Byfleet, displacing other vehicles to the Orpington area. By the time Tellings-Golden Miller was acquired by Travel London in June 2005, just four remained in use (985, 990-2).

Under the ownership of Travel London (the second attempt), the Excels operated on routes in the Surrey area. A livery of white and red was applied, with 990 being the first to gain this livery in July 2005. By the summer of 2006, they took up new rolling stock numbers E101-4. However, they left Byfleet shortly after, passing to Travel Dundee.

Tellings-Golden Miller inherited nine Optare Excels from Capital Logistics in June 1999. 991 (R991EWU) is seen awaiting time at Staines bus station before heading to Kingston on the 461. *Ian Armstrong Collection*

Travel London/Limebourne/Connex

National Express owned Travel West Midlands won two London contracts in 1998 (C1 and 211), both of which commenced in June of that year. The 211 (Hammersmith–Waterloo Station) saw twenty-one 9.6m Optare Excels taken into stock in May and June. No fleet numbers were carried by these vehicles, which were registered R401-5/7-22HWU. A livery of all-red, relieved by a white and blue diagonal stripe, was worn.

In August 2000, Travel London ceased to exist after National Express pulled out of London. The routes and vehicles passed to Limebourne under Independent Way ownership. Under the new operator, fleet numbers 301-305 and 307-22 were applied to the Excels. However, their time with Limebourne was short-lived, the latter operator being acquired by Connex in July 2001.

From this date, fleet numbers XL301-5/7-22 were applied to the Excels by Connex. The Excels continued operating the 211 under Connex ownership until November 2002, at which time the route gained a fleet of Dennis Tridents. After this, the Excels returned to National Express ownership, passing to either Travel West Midlands or Travel Dundee.

Travel London purchased twenty-one Optare Excel saloons for route 211 in 1998. R415HWU shows off the original livery applied to these buses. It is captured by the camera on layover in Hammersmith bus station. *Ian Armstrong Collection*

MARSHALL MINIBUS

The Marshall Minibus was one of the more unsuccessful midibuses to operate in London by far, with the majority only lasting just over two years.

Go Ahead London

London General took stock of fifteen Marshall Minibus saloons between September 1996 and January 1997. ML1 arrived first in September, being allocated to Putney for route C3 (Earls Court Station–Clapham Junction). It was followed by ML2 to ML6 in October, these again finding a home at Putney. Registration marks P501-6HEG were carried by these vehicles. A month later, in November, ML3 and ML5 were placed on loan to Sutton for a brief period, returning to their home garage in December.

ML7 to ML13 were allocated to Sutton upon arrival in November and December 1996, with ML14 and ML15 arriving in January 1997. They were shared between routes 413 (Sutton–Morden Station) and S1 (Beddington Corner–Banstead). The batch took up registration marks P407-15KAV. Members of this small batch of nine returned to Marshalls for modification work soon after arrival in late 1996. This led to the loan of a similar vehicle registered N776YAV, which was allotted temporary rolling stock number MS1. All fifteen gained Streetline names.

The first six Marshall Minibuses to be purchased by London General were allocated to Putney for use on the C3. The last of these, ML6 (P506HEG), is photographed at Clapham Junction. *Ian Armstrong Collection*

A larger batch
of nine Marshall
Minibuses were
allocated to Sutton
for use on routes
413 and S1. ML12
(P402KAV) is seen
on the latter route,
paused at Sutton
Post Office. *Ian
Armstrong Collection*

A larger batch of nine Marshall Minibuses were allocated to Sutton for use on routes 413 and S1. ML12 (P402KAV) is seen on the latter route, paused at Sutton Post Office. *Ian Armstrong Collection*

The Marshall Minibus had a short working life with Go-Ahead London, with all fifteen leaving London in April and May 1999, returning to Marshalls of Cambridge. Their place being taken by DRL-class Dennis Darts and MRL-class MetroRiders, displaced from Bexleyheath by the introduction of low-floor Dennis Dart SLFs.

MTL London

A solitary Marshall Minibus was delivered to MTL London Northern in November 1996. Allocated to Potters Bar garage, it was put to use on local town service PB1. Registered P481HEG, this vehicle was numbered MC1. It was transferred to the ownership of Metroline in August 1998 along with the MTL London Northern business. It remained operating for its new owner until 2002 when it was sold.

Centrewest/First London

Centrewest took stock of the largest batch – sixteen – of Marshall Minibus saloons. All were allocated to Greenford for use on routes in the Ealing and Greenford areas of West London. Numbered ML101 to ML116, registration marks R101-5, 706, 107-10, 211, 112-6VLX were carried by these vehicles. Delivery was drawn out over ten months. ML103 was first to arrive in November 1997, followed by ML101 and ML109 in December. January 1998 saw the arrival of ML108/13/4. A further two examples, ML104 and ML112, followed in February, with ML105 and ML107 in March. ML111/5/6 put in an appearance in May. The final members of the batch, ML102 and ML110, arrived in July and August respectively.

Like those operated by Go-Ahead London, the Centrewest Marshall Minibuses again had short careers in London, being withdrawn between March and September 1999, returning to Marshalls of Cambridge.

Limebourne

Limebourne took the first six of Go-Ahead London's Marshall Minibuses on loan in October 1997 for use on the C3. They retained fleet numbers ML1 to ML6 (P501-6HEG). The Streetline names were replaced by Limebourne fleet names.

Sixteen Marshall Minibuses were ordered by First London. They were allocated to Greenford garage for use on routes in the Greenford and Ealing areas. ML109 (R109VLX) represents the batch and is seen on layover in Greenford. *Ian Armstrong Collection*

October 1997 saw the C3 pass to Limebourne Travel. The six Marshall Minibus saloons used by London General on the route were loaned to Limebourne. ML2 (P502HEG) is photographed at Clapham Junction. *Ian Armstrong Collection*

MERCEDES-BENZ O814D

The Mercedes-Benz Vario model was first launched in 1996, being an updated version of the second-generation Mercedes-Benz minibuses. The model was a success around the country, featuring in many large and small operators' fleets.

First London

First London took stock of the first Mercedes-Benz O814D midibuses in London. A pair of Marshall bodied examples arrived in 1997 for use in the Orpington area. They were numbered MM25 and MM26 (P825/6NAV), with MM25 arriving in June 1997, followed by MM26 in August. MM25 was the first of the type to enter service in London. It was placed on loan at Uxbridge where it was used on the U2 before moving to Orpington for use on the R1.

Epsom Buses

A small batch of O814Ds arrived with Epsom Buses in October 1998 for use on routes K9 and K10, these services being supported by Surrey County Council. These were numbered 451 to 455 and carried registration marks S451-5LGN. One of these was

S455LGN represents the small batch of Plaxton Beaver 2 bodied Mercedes-Benz O814D midibuses operated by Epsom Buses. It is seen on route 404 to Caterham-on-the-Hill. *Ian Armstrong Collection*

employed on the 404 between Coulsdon and Caterham-on-the-Hill. Just prior to their arrival, a similar vehicle registered S313DLG was hired by the company. In January 2002, the Epsom Buses fleet was renumbered, with 451-5 taking new fleet numbers MB15-9. They were retained by Epsom Buses until August 2005; at which time they were sold for further use.

Stagecoach London

In the later months of 1997, eighteen Plaxton Beaver 2 bodied Mercedes-Benz O814Ds were taken into stock by Stagecoach London. Fourteen were allocated to Plumstead for routes 380 and 386, the other four went to Catford for route 273 (Lewisham–Grove Park). The first three arrived in October numbered MB8, 16/7 (R508YWC etc). These were the trio allocated to Catford. MB1, 2, 3, 13/4/8 (R501YWC etc) arrived in November, with MB4-7, 9-12, 15 (R504YWC etc) completing the batch in December. These were allocated to Plumstead.

The C1 (Victoria–Kensington) was sub-contracted to both Stagecoach SelKent and Metrobus on 28 February 1998. SelKent operated some of its MB-class O814D midibuses on its workings on the route, these operating from Plumstead. This was a short-lived arrangement, the C1 passing to Travel London on 13 June 1998.

In March 2001, route 273 was extended from Grove Park to Petts Wood Station. To cover this, MB2, 6, 7 and 15 transferred from Plumstead to Catford. They were also used on temporary service 584. The 273 was lost to First Centrewest in January 2002. After this date the MB-class midibuses at Catford were placed into store.

The type was withdrawn temporarily in February for safety inspections after a fault with similar vehicles operating with Stagecoach Manchester. To cover, Darts were used on the 380 for a few days before the O814Ds returned to service.

Eighteen Plaxton Beaver 2 bodied Mercedes-Benz O814D midibuses were purchased by Stagecoach London and allocated to the Selkent division. MB5 (R505YWC) is captured by the camera at Victoria whilst operating the C1. *Ian Armstrong Collection*

The MB-class operated by Stagecoach were intended for routes 273, 380 and 386. MB10 (R510YWC) is seen in Woolwich bound for Lewisham on the 380. *Ian Armstrong Collection*

The batch were re-numbered 42001-18 in January 2003. MB1-4, 13/4 had left London by this time. The others transferred to Manchester in May 2003. 42018 was the last of the type to operate in London.

Tellings-Golden Miller

A pair of Mercedes-Benz O814Ds with Plaxton Beaver 2 bodywork were taken into stock by Tellings-Golden Miller in 1998 and 1999. The first arrived in September 1998, taking up fleet number 707 (S707JJH). It was put to use on the Kingston University contract. Originally wearing corporate livery, it soon gained an all-over advertisement for Thames Radio, followed by a second for the Panasonic shop in Staines.

The second O814D was taken into stock registered S708TCF, this being numbered 708. It arrived in January 1999 and was put to use on the 471 (Kingston–Dittons–Hersham–Weybridge–Addlestone–New Haw–Woking Station). It operated the route alongside two Dart SLFs. The rolling stock numbers were added to these eight vehicles in 2003 when the fleet was numbered.

Tellings-Golden Miller won the contract for route 81 (Woking–Barnsbury Estate), as well as routes 437 and 438. Four Plaxton Beaver 2 bodied O814Ds were hired by the company from Dawson Rentals. These were registered S548, 954/7BNV and V258BNV. These were later numbered 748, 754/7 and 758 by Tellings-Golden Miller. The 437 was lost in November 2002, at which time 748 and 754 went on loan to Countryliner, the route passing to Thames Bus in December. The loaned vehicles returned in September 2003.

V258BNV was officially taken into stock by the company during November 2001, retaining rolling stock number 758.

Two Plaxton Beaver 2 bodied O814Ds were acquired from Crystals of Dartford in August 2003. Registered S107/8HGX, they took up fleet numbers 717 and 718. They joined 701-6 on the Orpington area routes. 717 sustained severe accident damage in September 2004. After repair, it went to Byfleet garage. 718 also experienced the same fate in December 2004. This too was repaired and returned to service. The sale of the Orpington operation to Metrobus in March 2005 meant that 718 transferred to Byfleet.

717, 748/9, 754/7/8 transferred to Travel London in June 2005, these operating from Byfleet on Surrey area services. They remained in use there until being sold.

Crystals, Dartford

The pair of Mercedes-Benz O814Ds mentioned above were taken into stock by Crystals in January 1999, both carrying Plaxton Beaver 2 bodywork. These were registered S107/8HGX and were used mostly on route R2 (Petts Wood–Orpington–Biggin Hill). As mentioned above, they were sold along with their routes to Tellings-Golden Miller in August 2003.

Tellings-Golden Miller operated 707 (S707JJH) on the Kingston University contract. It is seen wearing the dedicated livery for the route. *Matthew Wharmby*

MERCEDES-BENZ O810D

The Mercedes-Benz O810D was another variant of the Vario model introduced in 1996.

Tellings-Golden Miller

Tellings-Golden Miller took stock of six Mercedes-Benz O810Ds, all of which carried Plaxton Beaver 2 bodywork. The first four arrived in the summer of 1997 for use on Surrey County Council tendered services 501, 511 and 521, these being won from Westlink. Wearing the standard white with blue skirt and yellow band livery of Tellings-Golden Miller, P701-4MCF arrived in July 1997. These were followed in August by two more, registered R705/6MJH. By 2001, these midibuses had migrated on to routes 514, 515 and 564. Rolling stock numbers 701 to 706 were allotted to these vehicles.

701 to 706 moved to Dartford in August 2003 after the operations of Crystals were acquired. They were used on routes R2 (Petts Wood–Orpington–Biggin Hill) and R8 (Orpington–Biggin Hill). Just under a year later, the R2 gained a batch of Caetano Nimbus bodied Dart SLFs. By July 2004, 701-4 had moved to sister company Burtons of Haverhill.

P703LCF was one of four Plaxton Beaver 2 bodied Mercedes-Benz O810D minibuses taken into stock by Tellings-Golden Miller for use on routes into Surrey. It is photographed reversing off a bay at Kingston's Cromwell Road bus station. *Matthew Wharmby*

First Thamesway

First Thamesway also took stock of the Marshall bodied Mercedes-Benz O810D. Nine of the type arrived in September 1997 for routes 362 (King George Hospital–Barkingside Station) and 462 (Ilford–Hainault). R411-9VPU were numbered 411 to 419 by the company and were allocated to Ponders End garage. By June 2001, the 462 moved to Northumberland Park and had gained a fleet of Wright Handybus bodied Dennis Dart saloons. In September 1998, they moved on long-term loan to First Capital for further use, and subsequently passed to First London in October 2003. They left London in July 2004 or March 2005.

R411VPU was originally numbered 411 by First Thamesway. It is seen on layover at Chingford Station whilst operating route 379 to Yardley Lane Estate. *Ian Armstrong Collection*

Similar 415 (R415VPU) is seen on its intended route, the 362. It shows off the yellow and purple livery applied to the First Thamesway fleet. *Ian Armstrong Collection*

R413VPU was one of nine O810D midibuses to be placed on long-term loan to First Capital in September 1998. It was renumbered 573 and gained the 80 per cent red livery as seen above. *Ian Armstrong Collection*

Epsom Buses

Three UVG CitiStar bodied Mercedes-Benz O810D midibuses arrived at Epsom Buses in November 1997. These vehicles took registration marks R211-3MGT. They were put to use on route S4 (Sutton–Belmont–Wallington–Roundshaw) wearing the cream and maroon livery. The trio operated with Epsom Buses for five years before being sold for further use.

County Bus

County Bus took stock of a solitary Plaxton Beaver 2 bodied O810D which was allocated to Edmonton garage. Numbered MBV951, it took registration mark R951VPU. It arrived in April 1998, replacing MD602 which had caught fire, and was put to use on the W15 and W16. On 3 October 1998, Edmonton garage, along with routes and vehicles, transferred from Arriva East Herts & Essex (County Bus) to Arriva London.

OPTARE SOLO

The Optare Solo was one of the first low-floor midibuses, becoming a popular choice to replace the numerous 'bread van' type mini and midibuses that were in operation around the country. It first entered the market in 1998 and came in varying sizes. A Slimline version was introduced in 2004, this being one of the shortest at 7.8m. The SE model, introduced in June 2006, was the smallest, measuring 7.1m. Numerous London operators took stock of the type over the years, in small quantities at a time.

Travel London/Connex/Abellio London

Travel London was the first operator to take stock of the Optare Solo. Ten M850 models arrived in December 1998, registered S231-40EWU. Seating twenty-six, these vehicles were put to use on the C1 wearing a red livery, relieved by blue and white. Connex purchased the Travel London operation on 7 July 2001, with these vehicles transferring, taking up stock numbers S231-40.

Connex purchased eight additional M850 Solos registered YT51EAW/X/Y, EBA/C/D/F/G. These twenty-eight seaters were employed on the C3 (Earls Court–Clapham Junction) and followed on from the original fleet as S241-8. Four additional Solos were taken into stock during March 2002 for use on the C3. S249 to S252 were registered YP02LCA/C/E/F.

National Express purchased the operations of Connex in February 2004, with S231-252 passing to the new company. S231-40 were withdrawn in June 2005, passing to sister company Travel West Midlands at this time.

The C3 was converted to double-deck operation on 6 May 2006, at which time S241-7 went into storage, initially at Battersea, before moving for further storage at Beddington. August 2006 saw S241-4 transfer to the Travel Surrey operations based at Byfleet; S245/6 were withdrawn and sold whilst S247 transferred to Fulwell in September. S248-52 transferred to Walworth in June 2006.

The Travel London fleet was renumbered in March 2007 into a four-digit system similar to that used by parent company Travel West Midlands. The Optare Solos took up new rolling stock numbers 8841-4/7-52. Two of these, 8849 and 8851, did not last much longer with the company, being withdrawn in August 2007. The remaining Optare Solos were transferred to the Surrey operation at Byfleet in August 2008.

On 9 June 2009, Ned Railways acquired the business of Travel London, the company being rebranded Abellio London in October 2009. The remaining Optare Solos continued to operate under the new owners. These were withdrawn between 2012 and 2015.

Travel London was the first operator to take stock of the Optare Solo in London, these being used on the C1. S237EWU shows off the subtle route branding applied to the batch. *Ian Armstrong Collection*

S241 (YT51EAW) is photographed on layover at Clapham Junction whilst on the C3. It shows off the simplistic livery worn by the Solos under Connex ownership. *Ian Armstrong Collection*

Crystals, Dartford/TGM

Crystals of Dartford was the second operator to purchase the Optare Solo for use on routes in London. April 2000 saw the arrival of three Solos for use on Mobility routes in the Croydon area, these carrying registration marks W427/41/2CWX. The first of the trio was an M850 model seating thirty, the latter being M920s with a seating capacity of twenty-seven.

Five additional M850 models arrived in May 2001 for use on route B14 (Bexleyheath–Orpington Station). They carried registrations Y291/3-6PDN. An additional M850 Solo entered the fleet during November 2001. Registered YJ51JWW, this vehicle could seat twenty-nine passengers. Two similar saloons were taken into stock during January 2003 for use on a private contract for Guys and St Thomas Hospital. These wore an all-white livery, with NHS logos. These were registered MW52PYS and MW52PYT.

The operations and buses of Crystals were acquired by Tellings-Golden Miller in August 2003. They continued to operate the fleet of Solos until the 5 March 2005 when Metrobus acquired the Orpington operations of Tellings-Golden Miller.

Abellio's Optare
Solos were moved to the company's Byfleet garage where they were used on routes in Surrey. They were repainted into a white and red livery for use on these services. 8842 (YT51EAX) is photographed at Byfleet garage showing off this livery. *Liam Farrer-Beddall*

Orpington Station
finds Crystals Optare
Solo W427CWX.
It was one of three
new to the company
in 2000 for mobility
routes. *Ian Armstrong
Collection*

Orpington Station
also finds Y295PDN
blinded for St Mary
Cray Station on route
R6. It was new to
Crystals of Dartford
in May 2001. *Ian
Armstrong Collection*

First London/Essex

First Group operated a large number of Optare Solos across the country. The first experience of operating one in the London area came in November 2000 when T789KNW, an M920 model, was loaned to First Capital from the London Borough of Waltham Forest. It was allocated to Ponders End for its stay and was used on a service linking Chingford with the Lea Valley Leisure Centre. It wore an all-white livery, relieved by London Borough of Waltham Forest logos. It was allocated fleet number 789 for its stay.

Thirty-seven Optare Solos were allocated to the First Essex operation, being shared across a couple of garages. Eleven of these were allocated to the company's Romford garage and were used to convert route 193 (Romford Market–Country Park Estate) to low-floor. These were again examples of the M850 model. Registration marks EO02FLA-H/J/K, FKZ were allocated to these vehicles along with rolling stock numbers 501 to 511. Arriving in March 2002, they wore the First London red livery, displacing a fleet of Mercedes-Benz minibuses on the route to other First Essex garages. In 2004, they were renumbered into a five-digit numbering series. 501-11 became OS53101-11 and transferred to the main First London fleet in September 2004. The batch departed London during April 2007, the first six passing to First West Yorkshire, the others seeing further service with First Devon & Cornwall.

Six smaller M780 21-seater Solos were purchased by First London in March 2005. OOS53701-6 (LK05DYO, DXP/R-U) were allocated to Hackney garage for use on the W12. They displaced a fleet of Mercedes-Benz Vario minibuses, converting the W12 to low-floor operation. This batch left London in October 2010, passing to First Eastern Counties.

First Essex allocated eleven Optare Solo buses to the 193 in March 2002, these wearing the First London willow leaf livery. 504 (EO02FLD) represents the batch, seen passing through Romford. *Ian Armstrong Collection*

First London's Hackney Wick garage operated a small fleet of Optare Solos on the W12. OOS53703 (LK05DXR) is photographed departing Walthamstow Central bus station heading towards Wanstead. *Liam Farrer-Beddall*

F.E. Thorpe

F.E. Thorpe of Wembley purchased a pair of M850s in October 2001 for use on London Mobility routes in the Brent, Harrow and Ealing areas. They took up rolling stock numbers OSL1 and OSL2, registered YJ51JWY/Z. They were returned off lease in October 2008.

Mitcham Belle / Centra London

Mitcham Belle operated a fleet of five Optare Solos. The first four arrived in September 2001 registered KX51UCS-V. They were put to use on Kingston area service K5. Fleet numbers 050 and 057 were allocated to KX51UCS and UCV in April 2002.

Centra took over the Mitcham Belle operations in August 2004, the Optare Solos passing to this new operator, gaining fleet numbers OS1-4. X385VVY was taken into stock during 2004 by Centra and numbered OS5.

Docklands Minibus, Poplar

Docklands Minibus took a trio of Optare Solo M850s into stock during September 2002 for use on a service to the Beckton Tesco store. These vehicles were registered YG52DHJ/K/L, the latter gaining a pink and blue livery, whilst the other two operated in an all-white livery. They were joined by two more in June 2003, these being registered YG52TSV and TSX. The pair were acquired from Shephall Express of Stevenage. Once the Tesco contract ceased, the Solos returned off loan.

Epsom Buses/Quality Line

Epsom Buses/Quality Line were the largest operator of the Optare Solo in the Greater London area, with no less than thirty-three standard Solos being operated, alongside a fleet of eight Solo SRs, details of which can be found later in this book.

The first eleven arrived in November 2002 for use on routes S4 (Sutton–Roundshaw) and S7, these being the M850 model. Originally numbered OE1-11, they soon took stock numbers OP1-11 (YE52FHH/J-P/R/S/U). OP11 was soon re-registered from YE52FHU to YE52FGU. They entered service in an all-red livery.

An M920 registered MW52PZD was loaned to the company during July 2003, with the ability to seat thirty-three passengers.

Mitcham Belle's KX51UCU is photographed at Morden loading for its journey to Ham on the K5. *Ian Armstrong Collection*

Ten M850s arrived between July 2003 and January 2004. OP12 (YN03NXF) was first to arrive in July 2003, and was put to use on the 470 (Epsom–Colliers Wood). OP13 (YN53SWF) followed in October. Both of these vehicles could seat twenty-eight passengers. The other eight arrived in January 2004, following on as OP14-21 and were registered YN53SUF, SVK/L/O/P/R, ZXA/B. OP20 was built as a hybrid vehicle, and remained like this until August 2008 when it was converted back to standard diesel. However, OP20 had a number of issues, and to help out, Mitcham Belle loaned Solo KX51UCS to Quality Line in October 2006, retaining its fleet number OS1 for the duration of its stay.

Another type of Solo entered the Quality Line fleet in April 2009, this being the M880. This model seated twenty-four and was employed on the 463 (Coulsdon–Eastfields). Numbered OP23-30 (YJ09MHK-O/U/V/X), they replaced older Solos which in turn replaced Dart SLFs on Epsom routes.

In July 2011, Quality Line commenced operation of the K5 (Ham–Kingston–Morden) which they won from London United. A month earlier, in June, three Optare Solo M880s were taken into stock numbered OP31-3 (YJ11EJA/C/D). These 23-seaters took up service on the K5.

Five Solos were renumbered for use on Epsom area services in July 2014. OP12 (YN03ZXF) became EB03; OP14 (YN53SUF) EB04; OP15 (YN53SVK) became EB05. The final two, OP16 and OP17 (YN53SVL/O), became EB06 and EB07 respectively. At the same time, they received a silver livery along with new registration marks. EB03 became E3HRR; EB04 was re-registered to E4HRR, with EB05 taking new registration mark E5HRR. In early 2016 they were replaced by OP23/4 (YJ09MHK/L) which took

YE52FHN was originally numbered OE06 by Epsom Buses and was used for routes S4 and S7. It is seen operating route 470 carrying the Quality Line fleet name. *Ian Armstrong Collection*

OP14 (YN53SUF) is captured by the camera passing through a wet Sutton town centre on its way to Colliers Wood Station on the 470. In 2012 the 470 gained a batch of Solo SR saloons. *Liam Farrer-Beddall*

OP28 (YJ09MHU) was new to Epsom Buses for use on the 463. However, it is seen helping out on route K5 as it passes Cromwell Road Bus Station in Kingston. *Liam Farrer-Beddall*

OP32 (YJ11EJC) was one of three Optare Solos purchased by Epsom Buses for use on the K5. It is seen in Kingston on its way to Morden. *Liam Farrer-Beddall*

OP12 (YN03ZXF), along with four others, was taken off London duties in July 2014 and placed on local services in Epsom. For this, they were repainted into a silver livery and renumbered with EB prefixes. OP12 took new registration mark E3HRR and became EB03. It is seen in Epsom town centre on local service E5 to Watersedge. *Liam Farrer-Beddall*

new fleet numbers EB08/09, with OP25 (YJ09MHM) becoming EB10. The private registration marks were transferred to these vehicles, becoming E3-5HRR in fleet number order.

In July 2017, the Quality Line fleet was renumbered into the five-digit fleet numbering sequence already in use by London United and London Sovereign. EB01/3 became OS20215/6; EB06-10 took new fleet numbers OS20217-21. Rolling stock numbers OS20247-20254 were taken up by OP26-33.

The Optare Solo lasted until September 2020, at which time OS20248/9/53 were sold. The fleet was replaced by newer Enviro 200 MMCs.

Metrobus

The first Optare Solo to enter service with Metrobus arrived in October 2002, being an M850 model. YE52FGV gained rolling stock number 394 and was put to use on local services in the Edenbridge area. It wore a yellow livery, operating the routes on behalf of Kent County Council. 396 (LW52AFA) was a second M850, entering the fleet in January 2003. It entered service in the traditional blue and yellow livery worn by Metrobus vehicles and was used in the Lewes area.

It has already been mentioned above that, on 5 March 2003, Metrobus acquired the Orpington operations of Tellings-Golden Miller. Nine Optare Solos were acquired at this time, these being Y291/3-6PDN, YJ51JWW, W427/41/2CWX. Fleet numbers 191, 193-6, 192, 197-9 were allocated to these vehicles.

A pair of shorter M710SE Solos were taken into stock in December 2006 for use on the R8 (Orpington–Biggin Hill), replacing the pair of Mercedes-Benz 411CDI minibuses used on this service. These seventeen seaters were numbered 101 and 102 (YJ56WVF/G). They passed to Go-Ahead London in July 2014, and remained in use until the summer of 2017 when they were sold to Ensign Bus.

A pair of short Optare Solo M710SE saloons were purchased by Metrobus to replace a pair of Mercedes-Benz Sprinters on Orpington area route R8. The second of these, 102 (YJ56WVG), is photographed approaching Orpington town centre. *Liam Farrer-Beddall*

Metroline

Five Optare Solo M780 saloons arrived in June 2005, renewing the rolling stock on the H1/2/3 services in the Golders Green and Hampstead Heath areas. These vehicles took up rolling stock numbers NSM660-4 (YK05CCD/E/J/N/O). They were originally going to be numbered NSM218-222 but were among the first vehicles to be numbered into a new system introduced by Metroline, where all vehicles were numbered in one series. Allocated to Perivale, they replaced older step-entrance minibuses on the routes. However, the routes passed to Arriva the Shires in June 2006, after which time they were withdrawn from service. They were spared being sold after a use was found for them on commercial route 346 in Watford. They eventually left the fleet in February 2009.

Metroline took back operation of the H2 and H3 in June 2018, for which a batch of Optare Solo SRs were purchased. However, these were late in arriving and the fleet of Solos operated by Arriva London, mentioned below, were placed on loan. In November 2018, OS68 (YJ06YRP) was officially acquired by Metroline as a spare vehicle for the route. It was originally allocated to Cricklewood. OS68 was withdrawn in April 2021 and was placed into store, initially at Potters Bar before moving to Perivale. In November 2021 it moved back to Potters Bar where it acted as a spare vehicle for the PB1 local service.

NSM660 (YK05CCD) was one of five Optare Solos purchased by Metroline for use on the H1/H2/H3 services in the Hampstead area. After these services passed to Arriva the Shires in 2006, the Solos were eventually put to use on route 346 in Watford. NSM660 is captured by the camera on layover in Watford town centre. *David Beddall*

Arriva the Shires took over the H1/H2/H3 group of services from Metroline in June 2006, purchasing five Optare Solos for the route. 2471 (YJ06YRT) is seen on layover at Golders Green bus station before heading to East Finchley on the H3. *Liam Farrer-Beddall*

Arriva the Shires & Essex/Arriva London

Arriva the Shires & Essex was another operator to purchase a large number of Optare Solos for use around the company. In June 2006, five slim-line Solos were purchased for the take up of routes H1/2/3 from Metroline. Registered YJ06YRP/R/S/T/U, these midibuses were numbered 2468 to 2472. January 2016 saw the London operations of Arriva the Shires & Essex pass to Arriva London. The Solos transferred, taking up new fleet numbers OS68-72. After their loan to Metroline, these vehicles were withdrawn in April 2019.

Go-Ahead London

Go-Ahead London operated an Optare Solo registered MX09HHW, numbered OS1. It wore a silver livery, operating contract work around the Olympic Park. The only other Solos to be operated were 101 and 102, listed under the Metrobus heading above.

Hackney Community Transport

CT Plus operated the second largest number of Optare Solos in London, with twenty-seven being used in service. OS1 (YJ08XDH), an M950 model, was another Solo used on contract work for the Olympic Village. It operated tours of the site, starting from Stratford Station. It wore a blue livery and wore a 2012 logo. It remained in the fleet until November 2012.

Seven M780SE Solos were taken into stock during February 2010 for use on the W12. These followed on, numbered OS2 to OS8. These vehicles were registered YJ59NRN/O, YJ10EYF/G/H/K/L. Just under a year later, eight M880s were taken into stock for use on the W5 (Archway–Harringay), taken over from Metroline in February 2011. OS9 to OS16 (YJ60PFA/D/E/F/G/K/N/O) arrived in January, ready for the take up of the service. Two similar vehicles also entered the fleet in February 2011 for use on a contract for Guys and St Thomas Hospitals NHS Trust, taken over from Bliss Travel. These continued the fleet numbering sequence as OS17 and OS18 (YJ60LRX/Y).

In the opening months of 2012, nine M950s were taken into stock for route 309 (Bethnal Green–Canning Town). OS19 to OS27 took up registration marks YJ61MKA, YJ12GVR/T/U/V/W/X/Y/Z. The first arrived in February 2012, the rest following in March. These Solos were unusual in that they were built to dual-door layout.

OS2 (YJ59NRN) was the first of seven Optare Solos purchased by Hackney Community Transport for use on the W12. It is seen departing Walthamstow bus station before completing its journey. *Liam Farrrer-Beddall*

Archway finds
OS14 (YJ60PFK), one of eight Optare Solos purchased by Hackney Community Transport for use on the W5, taken over from Metroline in February 2011. *Liam Farrer-Beddall*

Route 309 was the only route in London to receive a fleet of dual-door Optare Solos, these being the only ones to operate to this layout. 1762 (YJ12GVY), originally numbered OS26, is seen at Canning Town bus station, starting its journey to Bethnal Green. Hackney Community Transport renumbered its fleet, the Solos being done in June 2020. During the Covid-19 pandemic, buses had their capacities seriously reduced, the Solos being reduced to ten. This was communicated to the public using the stickers on the entrance doors. *Liam Farrer-Beddall*

CT Plus renumbered its fleet into a four-digit sequence, the Solos being renumbered during June 2020. OS2-16 became 1740-54, with OS19-27 following on as 1755-63. By this time OS17/8 had been sold from the fleet.

On 26 August 2022, the CT Plus operation passed to Stagecoach ownership with the fleet of Optare Solos mentioned above transferring.

Stagecoach London

Like the other big groups mentioned above, Stagecoach took stock of a large number of Optare Solos for its provincial operations. Four of the original style Solo were loaned to Stagecoach London in 2020. The Covid-19 pandemic created the need for additional buses for school services in London. Stagecoach London took stock of Solos, Solo SRs and Enviro 200s to help achieve this. 47632/8/41/2 (CN58BYA/H/L/M) came on loan in August 2020 from Stagecoach South Wales Cwmbran garage. 47632/8 and 47642 were allocated to Bromley, whilst Barking took stock of 47641. With the exception of 47641, the other three returned to Wales in December 2020, with 47641 returning in February 2021.

The Covid-19 pandemic created the need for additional buses in London to help operate school journeys. Four Optare Solos were loaned to Stagecoach London from Stagecoach Wales. 47641 (CN58BYL) was one of the quartet. It is seen on its way to Grange Hill. This particular vehicle was restricted to carrying eleven passengers. *Steve Maskell*

Stagecoach acquired the business of Hackney Community Transport at the end of August, with twenty-four Optare Solos passing to the new owner. 47917 (YJ10EYH) was one of the Solos to be acquired and is seen in Walthamstow. *Liam Farrer-Beddall*

The Stagecoach Group acquired the London operations of CT Plus on 26 August 2022. Twenty-four Optare Solos were amongst the 159 vehicles acquired. 1740/1 (YJ59NRN/O) took rolling stock numbers 47809/10. Fleet numbers 47915-9 were allocated to 1742 to 1746 (YJ10EYF/G/H/K/L). 1747-63 (YJ60PFA/D/E/F/G/K/ N/O, YJ61MKA, YJ12GVR/T/U/V/W/X/Y/Z) were numbered 47983 to 47999.

MERCEDES-BENZ SPRINTER

The Mercedes-Benz Sprinter was a step back from the Optare Solo, being a van-derived minibus. Two different models were operated in London in very small quantities. Five of the 411CDI model were purchased between 2002 and 2004, with eight examples of the Sprinter City 45 model being operated in the capital.

First London

Three Koch bodied Mercedes-Benz Sprinter 411CDI minibuses were purchased by First London. These arrived during March 2002 with a seating capacity of thirteen. Registration marks LT02NVC/B/D were allocated to these vehicles which were numbered ES797 to ES799 by First. They were allocated to Hackney Wick where they were used on the 395 (Limehouse–Surrey Quays). The service took the buses through Rotherhithe Tunnel. They were withdrawn in April and May 2006.

ES797 (LT02NVC) represents the three Koch bodied Mercedes-Benz 411CDI minibuses purchased by First London for use on the 395, running through the Rotherhithe Tunnel. It is seen off route on the W12 in Walthamstow, heading towards Wanstead. *Matthew Wharmby*

Telling-Golden Miller / Metrobus

The other two 411CDI minibuses were purchased by Tellings-Golden Miller in July 2004. Numbered 1 and 2, these vehicles took up registrations BU04UTN and BU04UTP respectively. They were put to use on the R8 between Orpington and Biggin Hill. Less than a year later, on 5 March 2005, the pair transferred to Metrobus, along with Tellings-Golden Miller's Orpington operations. They were replaced in December 2006 by Optare Solos.

Go-Ahead London

Two demand responsive services were introduced to London during 2019. One of these was operated by Go-Ahead London in the Sutton area, gaining the name Go Sutton. This introduced the second type of Mercedes-Benz Sprinter to the streets of London. The Mercedes-Benz Sprinter City 45 had been introduced at various locations across the UK since 2015 as an attempt by bus companies to reduce operating costs in some areas on routes that were less patronised.

The first six were acquired in March 2019 from Evobus, Coventry. Numbered MB1-6, registration marks BT15KLZ, BL16GAO, BT66TZL/M and BN17JFV/X were carried. All had previously seen service around the UK, MB3 and MB4 previously operating for fellow Go-Ahead Group company Oxford Bus Company on a similar type of service in Oxford. The numbers were made up by MB7 and MB8, these being new vehicles registered BV19YKA and BV19YKB. Both of these arrived with the company during April 2019.

The Covid-19 pandemic of 2020, with the introduction of social distancing measures at the end of March, reduced the capacity of buses and coaches. The service carried on for a short time before being suspended on 28 May 2020, never to return. MB3 to MB8 passed to East Yorkshire Motor Services, also owned by the Go-Ahead Group. MB1 and MB2 were retained by Go-Ahead London for use in their Commercial Services department. The latter two minibuses were transferred to the Go-South West operation in April 2022.

WRIGHTBUS STREETLITE WF/DF

The Streetlite is an integral single-deck introduced by Wrightbus of Ballymena in 2010. Originally only available as the WF model (wheel forward), Wrightbus introduced the door forward model (DF) in 2011, followed by the Max model in 2012. Whilst the majority of the latter two models do not fall under the true definition of a midibus, the WF model does. However, a couple of batches of Streetlite DFs that were purchased by London operators fall into the category.

Go-Ahead London

Go-Ahead London was the first operator to take stock of the Streetlite and took examples of both the WF and DF model, both of which were classified WS by the company. Go-Ahead was the only London operator to take stock of the WF model from new, others listed taking second-hand models.

Route 462 was won in 2012 from Arriva London. This saw the introduction of nine 8.8m twenty-eight seat Streetlite WFs. WS1 to WS9 (LJ12CGF/G/K/O/U/V/X/Y/Z) were purchased for the route, and allocated to the former Blue Triangle garage in Rainham.

The first Wright Streetlite WFs to be operated by Go-Ahead London were allocated to Rainham garage for use on the 462. WS5 (LJ12CGU) is photographed at Ilford Broadway shortly before completing its journey. *Liam Farrer-Beddall*

Sixteen WFs arrived at Northumberland Park over the course of January and February 2015 to take up service on the 192. WS33-48 (SN64CTZ, CUA/C/G/H/J/K/O/U/V/W/X/Y, CVA-C) were a short-term measure, a second batch arriving in July 2015. These vehicles took up rolling stock numbers, WS49-64, along with registration marks SM15HWR-H/J/K, VJZ, VKA-E, WCK/L/N/O. WS49-57 arrived in July, whilst WS58-64 put in an appearance in August. This latter batch were fitted with fly wheels, making them more environmentally friendly. After their arrival, WS33-48 were returned to Wrightbus for resale, a number of which returned to London, operating with RATP London.

April 2017 saw the return of WS35/6/8 (SN64CUC/G/J) to Go-Ahead London. They were placed into the Commercial Services fleet and allocated to Silvertown. They were put to use on a contract between Stratford International, Stratford City and the 'HereEast', a campus located in the Queen Elizabeth Olympic Park. WS33 wore a dark grey livery, WS36 an orange and grey livery. The final member of the trio, WS38, wore a turquoise and grey livery.

The loss of the 462 to Stagecoach London in 2017 meant that WS1-9 transferred to the Metrobus operation at Green Street Green in May. They were put to use on services in the Orpington area.

Another batch of WFs were purchased in 2017 to cover routes 379 (Chingford–Yardley Lane Estate) and 424. The former route required two vehicles, with WS79 and WS80 (SK17HHE/F) being allocated to Northumberland Park for this service upon arrival in July. The allocation for the 424 arrived in August, being allocated to Putney. These followed on from the 379 batch, numbered WS81-6 (SK17HKA-F).

WS51-5 and WS64 transferred in September 2020 from Northumberland Park to Green Street Green. Again, they were used by the company on various routes in the Orpington area.

WS42 (SN64CUV) is seen entering Edmonton Green bus station on its way to Enfield on the 192. *Liam Farrer-Beddall*

WS50 (SM15HWF) was one of the second batch of Streetlite WFs taken into stock for the 192. It is captured by the camera entering Edmonton Green bus station. *Liam Farrer-Beddall*

Three of the original 192 batch of Streetlite WFs were re-acquired by Go-Ahead London in April 2017. They were allocated to Silvertown and were used on the Here East contract in the Stratford area. WS38 (SN64CUJ) is seen wearing a blue livery for the contract, passing through Stratford City. *Liam Farrer-Beddall*

In May 2021, former WS33/4/7/9, 41-3/5/7/8 returned to Go-Ahead London from RATP London. They were allocated to the Metrobus operation at Croydon. They continued to operate on the 463 as they did with RATP London.

London United

London United took stock of a solitary Streetlite WF in December 2015. Registered SN65OKM, this vehicle was numbered WS1 and was allocated to Park Royal garage. In March 2016, the RATP London fleet was renumbered into a five-digit series. WS1 became WS20274.

Quality Line

Ten of the original batch of Streetlite WFs owned by Go-Ahead London for route 192 were acquired by Quality Line in January 2016 for use on route 463 (Coulsdon South Station–Pollards Hill). They took up rolling stock numbers WS01 to WS10 (SN64CTZ, CUA/H/K/U/V/W/Y, CVB/C). In July 2017 they were renumbered to WS20264-73.

The above vehicles transferred in May 2021 back to Go-Ahead London where they gained their former rolling stock numbers. They continued to be used on the 463.

August 2017 saw six Wrightbus Streetlite WFs arrive at Putney for use on the 424. WS81 (SK17HKA) was the first of the batch, and is seen on its way to Fulham, having just crossed Putney Bridge. *Liam Farrer-Beddall*

WS20265 (SN64CUA) was new to Go-Ahead London for use on the 192. These were returned off lease in the summer of 2015. Coulsden provides the backdrop to WS20265, seen heading towards Coulsdon South on route 463. *Liam Farrer-Beddall*

Arriva London

Arriva London took stock of two batches of Streetlite DFs for their South London operations between October 2016 and August 2017. These were smaller than the majority of the type to operate in London, measuring 9.7m. The first twenty-two, SLS1-22 (LK66AMO/U/V/X, ANF/P/R/U-X, AOA-H/J/L-N), were delivered in October 2016. They were allocated to Norwood for use on route 450 between West Croydon and Lower Sydenham. SLS23-8 followed in July 2017, with SLS29/30 completing the batch in August. Registration marks SK17HJF/G/J/N/O/U/V/X were allotted to these vehicles. Norwood garage again took stock of the type, being used on route 410 (Crystal Palace–Wallington).

The majority of Wrightbus Streetlite DF saloons to operate in London exceeded the length of a midibus. However, Arriva London operated thirty, these being shared between routes 450 and 410. SLS1 (LK66AMO) is seen paused at West Croydon bus station. *Liam Farrer-Beddall*

Sullivan Buses

South Mimms based Sullivan Buses won the contract for route 299 (Southgate–Muswell Hill). Eight 9.7m Streetlite DFs arrived in January 2018 for use on the service. Fleet numbers SL90-7 were given to the vehicles, along with registration marks CP, JF, JJ, KT, LW, MH, PJ, SL67SUL. They were joined by a ninth vehicle, logically numbered SL98. This, however, was a 10.8m long version which carried registration mark SL15ZGR.

2017 saw Sullivan Buses take over the 299, purchasing eight of the 9.7m long Streetlite DFs. SL91 (JF67SUL) is seen loading at Southgate station before heading to Muswell Hill. *Liam Farrer-Beddall*

SM68ERZ was the only Wrightbus Streetlite DF operated by Tower Transit that measured below 10m in length. It was classified WM, whereas the main batch of Streetlite DFs were classified WVs by the company. Numbered WM46001, it is seen passing through Mile End on its way to Shadwell. *Liam Farrer-Beddall*

Tower Transit/Stagecoach London

Tower Transit was another London operator to take stock of the longer 10.8m Streetlite DF model. However, the company acquired a single Streetlite DF for route 339, this measuring 9.7m in length. Registered SM68ERZ, this vehicle took up stock number WM46001 when it arrived at Lea Interchange in December 2018.

The operations and vehicles operated by Tower Transit from its Lea Interchange garage were acquired by the Stagecoach Group in June 2022. WM46001 was one of the buses to transfer to Stagecoach. It gained new rolling stock number 39139 with its new owner.

Uno

Hatfield based Uno Buses purchased two batches of Streetlites in 2012 and 2018 respectively. Five WF models were used on routes in Hertfordshire, whilst a similar number of DF saloons were used on a couple of services linking Bedford and Milton Keynes. An eleventh Streetlite, another WF model, was added to the fleet in August 2020. Former Go-Ahead London SN64CVA was added to the Uno fleet, numbered WS46. It was acquired to help cover an increase in peak vehicle requirement on the 383, starting on 19 September 2020. It was also used on a duplicate school-time journey on the 395 in the Harrow area. The 383 was extended to Finchley Memorial Hospital at the end of October, leading to WS46 being mostly used on the route.

OPTARE SOLO SR

The Optare Solo SR was an updated version of the original Optare Solo model introduced October 2007. From January 2012 the SR model replaced the original Solo. A few London operators took small numbers of the type into stock to fulfil their small-bus requirements.

Quality Line

Quality Line was the first company to operate the type in the London area, with eight Solo SRs being purchased for use on TfL service 470 between Colliers Wood and Epsom. YJ62FUD/G, FVN/T, FWB, FXA/G/K were delivered in November 2012, taking stock numbers OPL01 to OPL08. Originally to have been numbered OPL34-41, these were of the M970SR model. Seating twenty-six passengers, these vehicles were built to dual-door layout. They were followed by the loan of a demonstration model registered YJ12NBX, this arriving in the early part of 2013.

Eight Optare Solo SRs were operated by Epsom Buses on route 470, these being new to the company in November 2012. OPL01 (YJ62FUD) is photographed at Morden station, showing off the dual-door layout.
Liam Farrer-Beddall

A handful of other Solo SRs were purchased by Quality Line between 2013 and 2016. First was OP34 (YJ13HJN), this being an M890SR model. It arrived in August 2013 and was put to use on the 404 (Coulsdon–Caterham-on-the-Hill). A pair of M900SR models followed in May 2014, this time for use on Surrey Commercial routes. YJ14BGK and BGO took up rolling stock numbers OP35 and OP36 upon arrival into the fleet, only to be renumbered EB01/02 in July 2014. June 2014 saw the arrival of a pair of M900SRs registered YJ14BGU/V. These also operated in the Epsom area, this time being employed on a contract for the NHS. YJ66ARO, an M9250SR model seating twenty-seven, was the final Solo SR to arrive with Quality Line, putting in an appearance in September 2016.

The Quality Line fleet was renumbered into a five-digit numbering series in July 2017, bringing them into line with the rest of the RATP London fleet. OPL01-08 became OS20256-20263; OP34 was renumbered OS20255; YJ14BGK/O taking new fleet numbers OS20215/6. YJ66ARO took up stock number OS20224. OS20256-63 were replaced on the 470 in December 2017 by a batch of short AD Enviro 200 MMCs. OS20255 was sold by RATP London in March 2019, with OS20215/6 leaving the fleet in June 2021. It was at this time that the contracts the pair had been working passed to Cobra Corporate.

Four more Solo SRs were purchased by Epsom Buses during 2014 for use on services in the Epsom area. EB02 (YJ14BGO) was one of these, photographed in Epsom town centre wearing the silver livery. *Liam Farrer-Beddall*

Metroline

Metroline won the contract for routes H2 and H3, taking over these services on 9 June 2018. A batch of six Optare Solo SR M7900SRs were ordered for the service but these were late in arriving. As has been mentioned under the Optare Solo section, the company took the batch of Optare Solos owned by Arriva London on loan to cover.

To assist Metroline with driver training, an M7800SR model registered YJ67GEK was loaned and operated in an all-white livery over the summer of 2018, returning to Optare in September. It was at this time that the intended batch of Solo SRs arrived at Cricklewood. Numbered OS2499 to OS2504, the vehicles were the smallest buses to operate on a TfL service at this time, seating a mere nineteen passengers. Registration marks YJ68FXA/B/F/C/E/G were allocated to this batch.

In June 2021, a Solo SR registered OP02ARE was taken into stock at Potters Bar. It was allocated rolling stock number OSE2750 but was never used by the company. It was returned to Optare the same month.

YJ67GEK was loaned to Metroline from Optare Limited to help the company with type familiarisation. It is seen on layover at Golders Green bus station. *Liam Farrer-Beddall*

OS2499 (YJ68FXA)
is captured by the
camera at Golders
Green shortly
before completing
its journey. *Liam
Farrer-Beddall*

Stagecoach London

Like the Optare Solo, Stagecoach London never purchased any Optare Solo SRs. It was the need for extra vehicles for school services that brought the type to Stagecoach London. Ten Optare Solo SRs were taken on loan from the provinces, working alongside the standard Optare Solos mentioned earlier in this book, as well as a fleet of Enviro 200s.

47847 and 47848 CN13CYT/U arrived from Stagecoach South Wales, being loaned from Aberdare garage. The other eight were loaned from Stagecoach East's Bedford garage. Seven of these were numbered 48024/5, 48031-5 (YJ15ANU/V, YJ66ARZ, ASO/U/V/X). The eighth vehicle was to have been 48036 (YJ66ASZ) but this Solo SR suffered engine failure whilst heading towards London. It was replaced by 48023 (YJ15AMR). 48024/5, 47847/8 were allocated to Barking; 48031/2 were allocated to West Ham. Kangley Bridge Road took stock of 48033/4, whilst 48023/35/6 were added to Plumstead's allocation. 48032 transferred in February 2021 from West Ham to

Nine Optare Solo SRs were loaned to Stagecoach London for extra school work during the Covid-19 pandemic. 48024 (YJ15ANU) was one of seven loaned from Stagecoach East. It is seen bound for Gants Hill on route 462. *Steve Maskell*

Plumstead. Further transfers took place in March. 48023/32/5 made the move between Plumstead and Bromley. At the same time 48031 moved from West Ham to Barking.

47847/8 returned to Stagecoach Wales in January 2021. The others left London in July. 48023/4/5/31 were re-allocated to Stagecoach Manchester, whilst 48032-5 returned to Stagecoach East.

MAN TGE

The MAN TGE minibus could be found operating a demand responsive style service in the London Borough of Ealing. M75094 (OV69DYN) is seen about to pass Ealing Broadway station. *Liam Farrer-Beddall*

The MAN TGE was a remodelled version of the Volkswagen Crafter van. Ten such vehicles were purchased by RATP London during 2019 for a new demand responsive service centred on the Ealing area of West London. These vehicles took up rolling stock numbers M75091 to M75100 and carried registration marks OV69DXU, DWK, DXC, DYN, DXM, OU69XPJ, OV69DWG, DVX, DWJ and DVZ. Allocated to Twickenham garage, M75091-100 arrived in London during October 2019 wearing a white and green livery. The service was branded as 'Slide Ealing' and was officially launched on 13 November 2019. Similar to the Go Sutton scheme operated by Go-Ahead London, the service was short lived as a result of the Covid-19 pandemic. The introduction of social distancing measures from 27 March 2020 meant that the service was suspended, the vehicles being returned off loan in June 2020.

M75098 (OV69DVX) was another of the MAN TGEs used on the Slide Ealing demand responsive service. It is seen at Ealing Broadway wearing a different livery to that worn by M75094 shown in the last photograph. *Liam Farrer-Beddall*

Appendix I
FLEET LISTS

The fleet lists in this section list the minibuses operated by each operator, with all types being listed under an operator rather than a type.

London Transport

BL1-95   **Bristol LH**   **ECW**

BL 1	KJD401P	BL20	KJD420P	BL39	KJD439P	BL58	OJD58R	BL77	OJD77R
BL 2	KJD402P	BL21	KJD421P	BL40	KJD440P	BL59	OJD59R	BL78	OJD78R
BL 3	KJD403P	BL22	KJD422P	BL41	OJD41R	BL60	OJD60R	BL79	OJD79R
BL 4	KJD404P	BL23	KJD423P	BL42	OJD42R	BL61	OJD61R	BL80	OJD80R
BL 5	KJD405P	BL24	KJD424P	BL43	OJD43R	BL62	OJD62R	BL81	OJD81R
BL 6	KJD406P	BL25	KJD425P	BL44	OJD44R	BL63	OJD63R	BL82	OJD82R
BL 7	KJD407P	BL26	KJD426P	BL45	OJD45R	BL64	OJD64R	BL83	OJD83R
BL 8	KJD408P	BL27	KJD427P	BL46	OJD46R	BL65	OJD65R	BL84	OJD84R
BL 9	KJD409P	BL28	KJD428P	BL47	OJD47R	BL66	OJD66R	BL85	OJD85R
BL10	KJD410P	BL29	KJD429P	BL48	OJD48R	BL67	OJD67R	BL86	OJD86R
BL11	KJD411P	BL30	KJD430P	BL49	OJD49R	BL68	OJD68R	BL87	OJD87R
BL12	KJD412P	BL31	KJD431P	BL50	OJD50R	BL69	OJD69R	BL88	OJD88R
BL13	KJD413P	BL32	KJD432P	BL51	OJD51R	BL70	OJD70R	BL89	OJD89R
BL14	KJD414P	BL33	KJD433P	BL52	OJD52R	BL71	OJD71R	BL90	OJD90R
BL15	KJD415P	BL34	KJD434P	BL53	OJD53R	BL72	OJD72R	BL91	OJD91R
BL16	KJD416P	BL35	KJD435P	BL54	OJD54R	BL73	OJD73R	BL92	OJD92R
BL17	KJD417P	BL36	KJD436P	BL55	OJD55R	BL74	OJD74R	BL93	OJD93R
BL18	KJD418P	BL37	KJD437P	BL56	OJD56R	BL75	OJD75R	BL94	OJD94R
BL19	KJD419P	BL38	KJD438P	BL57	OJD57R	BL76	OJD76R	BL95	OJD95R

BS1-17   **Bristol LHS**   **ECW**

BS 1	GHV501N	BS 5	GHV505N	BS 9	OJD9R	BS13	OJD13R	BS16	OJD16R
BS 2	GHV502N	BS 6	GHV506N	BS10	OJD10R	BS14	OJD14R	BS17	OJD17R
BS 3	GHV503N	BS 7	OJD7R	BS11	OJD11R	BS15	OJD15R		
BS 4	GHV504N	BS 8	OJD8R	BS12	OJD12R				

FS1-29 Ford Transit Various

FS 1	MLK701L	FS 7	MLK707L	FS13	MLK713L	FS19	MLK719L	FS25	CYT25V
FS 2	MLK702L	FS 8	MLK708L	FS14	MLK714L	FS20	MLK720L	FS26	CYT26V
FS 3	MLK703L	FS 9	MLK709L	FS15	MLK715L	FS21	GHM721N	FS27	C502HOE
FS 4	MLK704L	FS10	MLK710L	FS16	MLK716L	FS22	CYT22V	FS28	C503HOE
FS 5	MLK705L	FS11	MLK711L	FS17	MLK717L	FS23	CYT23V	FS29	C501HOE
FS 6	MLK706L	FS12	MLK712L	FS18	MLK718L	FS24	CYT24V		

Notes: FS1-20 were bodied by Strachan; FS22-6 were bodied by Dormobile; FS27-9 were new to London Buses Limited and carried Carlyle bodywork.

A list of the early small buses operated by London Transport can be found in appendix II.

London Buses Limited

CV1-7 CVE Omni CVE

CV1	F265WDC	CV3	F267WDC	CV5	A2LBR	CV6	A3LBR	CV7	A4LBR
CV2	F266WDC	CV4	F268WDC						

FM1-10 Iveco 49.10 Marshall

FM 1	K521DFL	FM 4	K524DFL	FM 6	K526DFL	FM 8	K528DFL	FM10	K530DFL
FM 2	K522DFL	FM 5	K525DFL	FM 7	K527DFL	FM 9	K529DFL		
FM 3	K523DFL								

FR1-7 Iveco 49.10 Reeve Burgess

FR1	H701YUV	FR3	H703YUV	FR5	H705YUV	FR7	H707YUV	FR8	H708YUV
FR2	H702YUV	FR4	H704YUV	FR6	H706YUV				

MA1-134 Mercedes-Benz 811D Alexander

MA 1	F601XMS	MA 16	F616XMS	MA 31	F631XMS	MA 46	F946BMS	MA 61	F661XMS
MA 2	F602XMS	MA 17	F617XMS	MA 32	F632XMS	MA 47	F947BMS	MA 62	F662XMS
MA 3	F603XMS	MA 18	F618XMS	MA 33	F633XMS	MA 48	F948BMS	MA 63	F663XMS
MA 4	F604XMS	MA 19	F619XMS	MA 34	F634XMS	MA 49	F949BMS	MA 64	F664XMS
MA 5	F605XMS	MA 20	F620XMS	MA 35	F635XMS	MA 50	F950BMS	MA 65	F665XMS
MA 6	F606XMS	MA 21	F621XMS	MA 36	F636XMS	MA 51	F951BMS	MA 66	F666XMS
MA 7	F607XMS	MA 22	F622XMS	MA 37	F637XMS	MA 52	F952BMS	MA 67	F667XMS
MA 8	F608XMS	MA 23	F623XMS	MA 38	F638XMS	MA 53	F953BMS	MA 68	F668XMS
MA 9	F609XMS	MA 24	F624XMS	MA 39	F639XMS	MA 54	F954BMS	MA 69	F669XMS
MA 10	F610XMS	MA 25	F625XMS	MA 40	F640XMS	MA 55	F955BMS	MA 70	F670XMS
MA 11	F611XMS	MA 26	F626XMS	MA 41	F641XMS	MA 56	F656XMS	MA 71	F671XMS
MA 12	F612XMS	MA 27	F627XMS	MA 42	F642XMS	MA 57	F657XMS	MA 72	F672XMS
MA 13	F613XMS	MA 28	F628XMS	MA 43	F643XMS	MA 58	F658XMS	MA 73	F673XMS
MA 14	F614XMS	MA 29	F629XMS	MA 44	F644XMS	MA 59	F659XMS	MA 74	F674XMS
MA 15	F615XMS	MA 30	F630XMS	MA 45	F645XMS	MA 60	F660XMS	MA 75	F675XMS

MA 76	F676XMS	MA 88	F688XMS	MA100	F700XMS	MA112	G112PGT	MA124	G124PGT
MA 77	F677XMS	MA 89	F689XMS	MA101	F701XMS	MA113	G113PGT	MA125	H425XGK
MA 78	F678XMS	MA 90	F690XMS	MA102	F702XMS	MA114	G114PGT	MA126	H426XGK
MA 79	F679XMS	MA 91	F691XMS	MA103	F703XMS	MA115	G115PGT	MA127	H427XGK
MA 80	F680XMS	MA 92	F692XMS	MA104	F704XMS	MA116	G116PGT	MA128	H428XGK
MA 81	F681XMS	MA 93	F693XMS	MA105	F705XMS	MA117	G117PGT	MA129	H429XGK
MA 82	F682XMS	MA 94	F694XMS	MA106	F706XMS	MA118	G118PGT	MA130	H430XGK
MA 83	F683XMS	MA 95	F695XMS	MA107	F707XMS	MA119	G119PGT	MA131	H431XGK
MA 84	F684XMS	MA 96	F696XMS	MA108	G108PGT	MA120	G120PGT	MA132	H432XGK
MA 85	F685XMS	MA 97	F697XMS	MA109	G109PGT	MA121	G121PGT	MA133	H433XGK
MA 86	F686XMS	MA 98	F698XMS	MA110	G110PGT	MA122	G122PGT	MA134	H434XGK
MA 87	F687XMS	MA 99	F699XMS	MA111	G111PGT	MA123	G123PGT		

MC1-5   Mercedes-Benz 811D   Carlyle

MC1	F430BOP	MC2	H882LOX	MC3	H883LOX	MC4	H884LOX	MC5	H885LOX

MR1-134   MCW MetroRider   MCW

MR 1	D461PON	MR 27	E127KYW	MR 53	E929KYR	MRL 79	F183YDA	MR105	F105YVP
MR 2	D462PON	MR 28	E128KYW	MR 54	E930KYR	MRL 80	F184YDA	MR106	F106YVP
MR 3	D463PON	MR 29	E129KYW	MR 55	E631KYW	MRL 81	F185YDA	MR107	F107YVP
MR 4	D464PON	MR 30	E130KYW	MR 56	E632KYW	MRL 82	F186YDA	MR108	F108YVP
MR 5	D465PON	MR 31	E131KYW	MR 57	E633KYW	MRL 83	F187YDA	MR109	F109YVP
MR 6	D466PON	MR 32	E132KYW	MR 58	E634KYW	MRL 84	F188YDA	MR110	F110YVP
MR 7	D467PON	MR 33	E133KYW	MR 59	E635KYW	MRL 85	F189YDA	MR111	F111YVP
MR 8	D468PON	MR 34	E134KYW	MR 60	E636KYW	MRL 86	F190YDA	MR109	F109YVP
MR 9	D469PON	MR 35	E135KYW	MR 61	E637KYW	MRL 87	F191YDA	MR110	F110YVP
MR 10	D470PON	MR 36	E136KYW	MR 62	E638KYW	MRL 88	F192YDA	MR111	F111YVP
MR 11	D471PON	MR 37	E137KYW	MR 63	E639KYW	MRL 89	F193YDA	MR109	F109YVP
MR 12	D472PON	MR 38	E138KYW	MR 64	E640KYW	MRL 90	F194YDA	MR110	F110YVP
MR 13	D473PON	MR 39	E139KYW	MRL 65	E641KYW	MRL 91	F195YDA	MR111	F111YVP
MR 14	D474PON	MR 40	E140KYW	MRL 66	E642KYW	MRL 92	F196YDA	MR109	F109YVP
MR 15	D475PON	MR 41	E141KYW	MRL 67	E643KYW	MRL 93	E873NJD	MR110	F110YVP
MR 16	D476PON	MR 42	E142KYW	MRL 68	E644KYW	MRL 94	E874NJD	MR111	F111YVP
MR 17	D477PON	MR 43	E143KYW	MRL 69	E645KYW	MRL 95	F895OYR	MR112	F112YVP
MR 18	D478PON	MR 44	E144KYW	MRL 70	E646KYW	MRL 96	F896OYR	MR113	F113YVP
MR 19	D479PON	MR 45	E145KYW	MRL 71	E647KYW	MRL 97	F897OYR	MR114	F114YVP
MR 20	D480PON	MR 46	E146KYW	MRL 72	E648KYW	MRL 98	F898OYR	MR115	F115YVP
MR 21	D481PON	MR 47	E147KYW	MRL 73	E649KYW	MR 99	F99YVP	MR116	F116YVP
MR 22	D482PON	MR 48	E148KYW	MRL 74	E650KYW	MR100	F100YVP	MR117	F117YVP
MR 23	E123KYW	MR 49	E149KYW	MRL 75	E705LYU	MR101	F101YVP	MR118	F118YVP
MR 24	E124KYW	MR 50	E150KYW	MRL 76	E706LYU	MR102	F102YVP	MR119	F119YVP
MR 25	E125KYW	MR 51	E151KYW	MRL 77	F197YDA	MR103	F103YVP	MR120	F120YVP
MR 26	E126KYW	MR 52	E152KYW	MRL 78	F182YDA	MR104	F104YVP	MR121	F121YVP

MR122	F122YVP	MR125	F125YVP	MR128	F128YVP	MR131	F131YVP	MR134	D482NOX
MR123	F123YVP	MR126	F126YVP	MR129	F129YVP	MR132	F132YVP		
MR124	F124YVP	MR127	F127YVP	MR130	F130YVP	MR133	F133YVP		

MRL135-241   Optare MetroRider   Optare

MRL135	H135TGO	MRL157	H157UUA	MRL179	H679YGO	MRL201	J701CGK	MRL223	K223MGT
MRL136	H136UUA	MRL158	H158UUA	MRL180	H680YGO	MRL202	J702CGK	MRL224	K424HWY
MRL137	H137UUA	MRL159	H159UUA	MRL181	H681YGO	MRL203	J703CGK	MRL225	K425HWY
MRL138	H138UUA	MRL160	H160WWT	MRL182	H682YGO	MRL204	J704CGK	MRL226	K426HWY
MRL139	H139UUA	MRL161	H161WWT	MRL183	H683YGO	MRL205	J705CGK	MRL227	K427HWY
MRL140	H140UUA	MRL162	H162WWT	MRL184	H684YGO	MRL206	J706CGK	MRL228	K428HWY
MRL141	H141UUA	MRL163	H163WWT	MRL185	H685YGO	MRL207	J707CGK	MRL229	K429HWY
MRL142	H142UUA	MRL164	H564WWR	MRL186	H686YGO	MRL208	J708CGK	MRL230	K430HWY
MRL143	H143UUA	MRL165	H165WWT	MRL187	H687YGO	MRL209	J709CGK	MRL231	K431HWY
MRL144	H144UUA	MRL166	H166WWT	MRL188	H688YGO	MRL210	J210BWU	MRL232	K432HWY
MRL145	H145UUA	MRL167	H167WWT	MRL189	H689YGO	MRL211	J211BWU	MRL233	K433HWY
MRL146	H146UUA	MRL168	H168WWT	MRL190	H690YGO	MRL212	J212BWU	MRL234	K434HWY
MRL147	H147UUA	MRL169	H169WWT	MRL191	J691CGK	MRL213	J213BWU	MRL235	K435HWY
MRL148	H148UUA	MRL170	H170WWT	MRL192	J692CGK	MRL214	J214BWU	MRL236	K436HWY
MRL149	H149UUA	MRL171	H171WWT	MRL193	J693CGK	MRL215	J215BWU	MRL237	K437HWY
MRL150	H150UUA	MRL172	H172WWT	MRL194	J694CGK	MRL216	J216BWU	MRL238	K438HWY
MRL151	H151UUA	MRL173	H173WWT	MRL195	J695CGK	MRL217	J217BWU	MRL239	K439HWY
MRL152	H152UUA	MRL174	H174WWT	MRL196	J696CGK	MRL218	J218BWU	MRL240	K440HWY
MRL153	H153UUA	MRL175	H175WWT	MRL197	J697CGK	MRL219	J219BWU	MRL241	K441HWY
MRL154	H154UUA	MRL176	H176WWT	MRL198	J698CGK	MRL220	J220BWU		
MRL155	H155UUA	MRL177	H677YGO	MRL199	J699CGK	MRL221	J221BWU		
MRL156	H156UUA	MRL178	H678YGO	MRL200	J710CGK	MRL222	K422HWY		

MT1-8   Mercedes-Benz 709D   Reeve Burgess

| MT1 | F391DHL | MT3 | F393DHL | MT5 | F395DHL | MT7 | G537GBD | MT8 | G538GBD |
| MT2 | F392DHL | MT4 | F394DHL | MT6 | F396DHL | | | | |

MTL1-5   Mercedes-Benz 811D   Reeve Burgess

| MTL1 | G621XLO | MTL2 | G622KWE | MTL3 | H189RWF | MTL4 | H191RWF | MTL5 | H192RWF |

MW1-37   Mercedes-Benz 811D   Wright

MW 1	HDZ2601	MW 6	HDZ2606	MW11	HDZ2611	MW16	HDZ2616	MW21	NDZ7921
MW 2	HDZ2602	MW 7	HDZ2607	MW12	HDZ2612	MW17	LDZ9017	MW22	NDZ7922
MW 3	HDZ2603	MW 8	HDZ2608	MW13	HDZ2613	MW18	NDZ7918	MW23	NDZ7923
MW 4	HDZ2604	MW 9	HDZ2609	MW14	HDZ2614	MW19	NDZ7919	MW24	NDZ7924
MW 5	HDZ2605	MW10	HDZ2610	MW15	HDZ2615	MW20	NDZ7920	MW25	NDZ7925

MW26	NDZ7926	MW29	NDZ7929	MW32	NDZ7932	MW34	NDZ7934	MW36	NDZ7936
MW27	NDZ7927	MW30	NDZ7930	MW33	NDZ7933	MW35	NDZ7935	MW37	NDZ7937
MW28	NDZ7928	MW31	NDZ7931						

OV1-52   Volkswagen LT55   Optare CityPacer

OV 1	C525DYM	OV12	D344JUM	OV23	D355JUM	OV34	D366JUM	OV45	D377JUM
OV 2	C526DYT	OV13	D345JUM	OV24	D356JUM	OV35	D367JUM	OV46	D378JUM
OV 3	C527DYT	OV14	D346JUM	OV25	D357JUM	OV36	D368JUM	OV47	D379JUM
OV 4	C528DYT	OV15	D347JUM	OV26	D358JUM	OV37	D369JUM	OV48	D380JUM
OV 5	D529FYL	OV16	D348JUM	OV27	D359JUM	OV38	D370JUM	OV49	D381JUM
OV 6	D338JUM	OV17	D349JUM	OV28	D360JUM	OV39	D371JUM	OV50	E998TWU
OV 7	D339JUM	OV18	D350JUM	OV29	D361JUM	OV40	D372JUM	OV51	E99TWU
OV 8	D340JUM	OV19	D351JUM	OV30	D362JUM	OV41	D373JUM	OV52	E638TWW
OV 9	D341JUM	OV20	D352JUM	OV31	D363JUM	OV42	D374JUM		
OV10	D342JUM	OV21	D353JUM	OV32	D364JUM	OV43	D375JUM		
OV11	D343JUM	OV22	D354JUM	OV33	D365JUM	OV44	D376JUM		

RB1-35   Renault S50   Reeve Burgess

RB 1	G871WML	RB 8	G878WML	RB15	G885WML	RB22	G892WML	RB29	H129AML
RB 2	G872WML	RB 9	G879WML	RB16	G886WML	RB23	G893WML	RB30	H130AML
RB 3	G873WML	RB10	G880WML	RB17	G887WML	RB24	G894WML	RB31	H131AML
RB 4	G874WML	RB11	G881WML	RB18	G888WML	RB25	G895WML	RB32	H132AML
RB 5	G875WML	RB12	G882WML	RB19	G889WML	RB26	H126AML	RB33	H133AML
RB 6	J876WML	RB13	G883WML	RB20	G890WML	RB27	H127AML	RB34	J134HME
RB 7	G877WML	RB14	G884WML	RB21	G891WML	RB28	H128AML	RB35	L235LLK

RH1-24   Iveco 49.10   Robin Hood

RH 1	C501DYM	RH 6	C506DYM	RH11	C511DYM	RH16	C516DYM	RH21	C521DYM
RH 2	C502DYM	RH 7	C507DYM	RH12	C512DYM	RH17	C517DYM	RH22	D522FYL
RH 3	C503DYM	RH 8	C508DYM	RH13	D513FYL	RH18	C518DYM	RH23	C523DYM
RH 4	C504DYM	RH 9	C509DYM	RH14	D514FYL	RH19	C519DYM	RH24	D524FYL
RH 5	C505DYM	RH10	C510DYM	RH15	C515DYM	RH20	C520DYM		

RW1-90   Renault S50   Wright

RW 1	HDZ5401	RW 7	HDZ5407	RW13	HDZ5413	RW19	HDZ5419	RW25	HDZ5425
RW 2	HDZ5402	RW 8	HDZ5408	RW14	HDZ5414	RW20	HDZ5420	RW26	HDZ5426
RW 3	HDZ5403	RW 9	HDZ5409	RW15	HDZ5415	RW21	HDZ5421	RW27	HDZ5427
RW 4	HDZ5404	RW10	HDZ5410	RW16	HDZ5416	RW22	HDZ5422	RW28	HDZ5428
RW 5	HDZ5405	RW11	HDZ5411	RW17	HDZ5417	RW23	HDZ5423	RW29	HDZ5429
RW 6	HDZ5406	RW12	HDZ5412	RW18	HDZ5418	RW24	HDZ5424	RW30	HDZ5430

RW31	HDZ5431	RW43	HDZ5443	RW55	HDZ5455	RW67	HDZ5467	RW79	HDZ5479
RW32	HDZ5432	RW44	HDZ5444	RW56	HDZ5456	RW68	HDZ5468	RW80	HDZ5480
RW33	HDZ5433	RW45	HDZ5445	RW57	HDZ5457	RW69	HDZ5469	RW81	HDZ5481
RW34	HDZ5434	RW46	HDZ5446	RW58	HDZ5458	RW70	HDZ5470	RW82	HDZ5482
RW35	HDZ5435	RW47	HDZ5447	RW59	HDZ5459	RW71	HDZ5471	RW83	HDZ5483
RW36	HDZ5436	RW48	HDZ5448	RW60	HDZ5460	RW72	HDZ5472	RW84	HDZ5484
RW37	HDZ5437	RW49	HDZ5449	RW61	HDZ5461	RW73	HDZ5473	RW85	HDZ5485
RW38	HDZ5438	RW50	HDZ5450	RW62	HDZ5462	RW74	HDZ5474	RW86	HDZ5486
RW39	HDZ5439	RW51	HDZ5451	RW63	HDZ5463	RW75	HDZ5475	RW87	HDZ5487
RW40	HDZ5440	RW52	HDZ5452	RW64	HDZ5464	RW76	HDZ5476	RW88	HDZ5488
RW41	HDZ5441	RW53	HDZ5453	RW65	HDZ5465	RW77	HDZ5477	RW89	HDZ5489
RW42	HDZ5442	RW54	HDZ5454	RW66	HDZ5466	RW78	HDZ5478	RW90	HDZ5490

SC1	D585OOV	Freight Rover Sherpa	Carlyle
SD1	D811KWT	Freight Rover Sherpa	Dormobile
SD2	D212GLJ	Freight Rover Sherpa	Dormobile

SR1-134 Mercedes-Benz 811D Optare StarRider

SR 1	E711LYU	SR 26	F926YWY	SR 51	F51CWY	SR 76	F176FWY	SR101	G101KUB
SR 2	E712LYU	SR 27	F927YWY	SR 52	F52CWY	SR 77	F177FWY	SR102	G102KUB
SR 3	E713LYU	SR 28	F928YWY	SR 53	F53CWY	SR 78	F178FWY	SR103	G103KUB
SR 4	E714LYU	SR 29	F29CWY	SR 54	F154FWY	SR 79	F179FWY	SR104	G104KUB
SR 5	F905YWY	SR 30	F30CWY	SR 55	F155FWY	SR 80	F180FWY	SR105	G105KUB
SR 6	F906YWY	SR 31	F31CWY	SR 56	F156FWY	SR 81	F181FWY	SR106	G106KUB
SR 7	F907YWY	SR 32	F32CWY	SR 57	F157FWY	SR 82	G82KUB	SR107	G107KUB
SR 8	F908YWY	SR 33	F33CWY	SR 58	F158FWY	SR 83	G83KUB	SR108	G108KUB
SR 9	F909YWY	SR 34	F34CWY	SR 59	F159FWY	SR 84	G84KUB	SR109	G109KUB
SR 10	F910YWY	SR 35	F35CWY	SR 60	F160FWY	SR 85	G85KUB	SR110	G110KUB
SR 11	F911YWY	SR 36	F36CWY	SR 61	F161FWY	SR 86	G86KUB	SR111	G111KUB
SR 12	F912YWY	SR 37	F37CWY	SR 62	F162FWY	SR 87	G87KUB	SR112	G112KUB
SR 13	F913YWY	SR 38	F38CWY	SR 63	F163FWY	SR 88	G88KUB	SR113	G113KUB
SR 14	F914YWY	SR 39	F39CWY	SR 64	F164FWY	SR 89	G89KUB	SR114	G114KUB
SR 15	F915YWY	SR 40	F40CWY	SR 65	F165FWY	SR 90	G90KUB	SR115	G115KUB
SR 16	F916YWY	SR 41	F41CWY	SR 66	F166FWY	SR 91	G91KUB	SR116	G116KUB
SR 17	F917YWY	SR 42	F42CWY	SR 67	F167FWY	SR 92	G92KUB	SR117	G117KUB
SR 18	F918YWY	SR 43	F43CWY	SR 68	F168FWY	SR 93	G93KUB	SR118	G118KUB
SR 19	F919YWY	SR 44	F44CWY	SR 69	F169FWY	SR 94	G94KUB	SR119	G119KUB
SR 20	F920YWY	SR 45	F45CWY	SR 70	F170FWY	SR 95	G95KUB	SR120	G120KUB
SR 21	F921YWY	SR 46	F46CWY	SR 71	F171FWY	SR 96	G96KUB	SR121	G121KUB
SR 22	F922YWY	SR 47	F47CWY	SR 72	F172FWY	SR 97	G97KUB	SR122	G122SMV
SR 23	F923YWY	SR 48	F48CWY	SR 73	F173FWY	SR 98	G98KUB	SR123	G123SMV
SR 24	F924YWY	SR 49	F49CWY	SR 74	F174FWY	SR 99	G99KUB		
SR 25	F925YWY	SR 50	F50CWY	SR 75	F175FWY	SR100	G100KUB		

Arriva London

SLS1-30   **Wrightbus Streetlite DF**   **Wright**

SLS 1	LK66AMO	SLS 7	LK66ANR	SLS13	LK66AOC	SLS19	LK66AOJ	SLS25	SK17HJJ
SLS 2	LK66AMU	SLS 8	LK66ANU	SLS14	LK66AOD	SLS20	LK66AOL	SLS26	SK17HJN
SLS 3	LK66AMV	SLS 9	LK66ANV	SLS15	LK66AOE	SLS21	LK66AOM	SLS27	SK17HJO
SLS 4	LK66AMX	SLS10	LK66ANX	SLS16	LK66AOF	SLS22	LK66AON	SLS28	SK17HJU
SLS 5	LK66ANF	SLS11	LK66AOA	SLS17	LK66AOG	SLS23	SK17HJF	SLS29	SK17HJV
SLS 6	LK66ANP	SLS12	LK66AOB	SLS18	LK66AOH	SLS24	SK17HJG	SLS30	SK17HJX

Arriva the Shires/Arriva London

2468-72   **Optare Solo**   **Optare**

2468	YJ06YRP	2469	YJ06YRR	2470	YJ06YRS	2471	YJ06YRT	2472	YJ06YRU

The above Optare Solos were transferred to Arriva London in 2016 where they were renumbered OS68 to OS72.

Capital Citybus

601-620   **Mercedes-Benz 811D**   **Reeve Burgess Beaver**

601	J601HMF	605	J605HMF	609	J609HMF	613	J613HMF	617	J617HMF
602	J602HMF	606	J606HMF	610	J610HMF	614	J614HMF	618	J618HMF
603	J603HMF	607	J607HMF	611	J611HMF	615	J615HMF	619	J619HMF
604	J604HMF	608	J608HMF	612	J612HMF	616	J616HMF	620	J620HMF

621-630   **Optare MetroRider**   **Optare**

621	J621HMH	623	J623HMH	625	J625HMH	627	J627HMH	629	J629HMH
622	J622HMH	624	J624HMH	626	J626HMH	628	J628HMH	630	J630HMH

631-3   **Mercedes-Benz 811D**   **Alexander**

631	J631HMH	632	J632HMH	633	J633HMH

671-680   **Volvo B6**   **Alexander Dash**

671	L671RMD	673	L673RMD	675	L675RMD	677	L677RMD	679	L679RMD
672	L672RMD	674	L674RMD	676	L676RMD	678	L678RMD	680	L680RMD

670/81-6   **Volvo B6**   **Northern Counties**

670	L670SMC	682	L888TJC	684	L4GML	685	L5GML	686	L6GML
681	L281RML	683	L888AMY						

701-4 Optare Excel Optare

701	P701HMT	702	P702HMT	703	P703HMT	704	P704HMT

Capital Logistics/Tellings-Golden Miller

Optare Excel Optare

R985EWU	R987EWU	R988EWU	R989EWU	R990EWU	R991EWU	R992EWU	R993EWU
R986EWU							

1	BU04UTN	Mercedes-Benz 411 Sprinter
2	BU04UTP	Mercedes-Benz 411 Sprinter

701-6 Mercedes-Benz O810D Plaxton Beaver 2

	P701LCF		P703LCF		P704LCF	705	R705MJH	706	R706MJH
	P702LCF								

707	S707JJH	Mercedes-Benz Vario 0814D	Plaxton Beaver 2
708	S708TCF	Mercedes-Benz Vario 0814D	Plaxton Beaver 2

Mercedes-Benz 709D Plaxton Beaver

	P70TGM		M70TGM		M80TGM		M90TGM		N70TGM
	M60TGM								

Connex

S241-252 Optare Solo Optare

S241	YT51EAW	S244	YT51EBA	S247	YT51EBF	S249	YP02LCA	S251	YP02LCE
S242	YT51EAX	S245	YT51EBC	S248	YT51EBG	S250	YP02LCC	S252	YP02LCF
S243	YT51EAY	S246	YT51EBD						

Crystals

	CSU909	Mercedes-Benz 609D	Crystals
	P348HKU	Mercedes-Benz 711D	Crystals
	CSU908	Mercedes-Benz 609D	Made-to-Measure
	S107HGX	Mercedes-Benz Vario	Plaxton Beaver
	S108HGX	Mercedes-Benz Vario	Plaxton Beaver
	P347HKU	Mercedes-Benz 711D	Crystals
	N601JGP	Mercedes-Benz 811D	Crystals

	N602JGP	Mercedes-Benz 811D	Crystals
	N603JGP	Mercedes-Benz 811D	Crystals
	N604JGP	Mercedes-Benz 811D	Crystals
	N605JGP	Mercedes-Benz 811D	Crystals
	N606JGP	Mercedes-Benz 811D	Crystals
	F921MTM	Mercedes-Benz 709D	Robin Hood

Optare Solo   **Optare**

	W427CWX		Y291PDN		Y294PDN		Y296PDN		MW52PYT
	W441CWX		Y293PDN		Y295PDN		MW52PYS		YJ51JWW
	W442CWX								

Docklands Buses

367-409   **Mercedes-Benz 811D**   **Carlyle**

367	H985FTT	390	H781GTA	398	H789GTA	402	H103HDV	406	H107HDV
368	H986FTT	393	H784GTA	399	H790GTA	403	H104HDV	407	H108HDV
370	H988FTT	394	H785GTA	400	H101HDV	404	H105HDV	408	H109HDV
371	H989FTT	395	H786GTA	401	H102HDV	405	H106HDV	409	H110HDV
389	H180GTA								

Eastern National/Thamesway/First Essex

600-604   **Ford Transit**   **Carlyle**

600	C600NPU	601	C601NPU	602	C602NPU	603	C603NPU	604	C604NPU

245-804   **Mercedes-Benz 709D**   **Reeve Burgess**

245	F245MVW	253	F253RHK	301	H301LPU	390	H390MAR	398	K398KHJ
246	F246MVW	254	F254RHK	302	H302LPU	391	H391MAR	800	F800RHK
247	F247NJN	255	F255RHK	303	H303LPU	392	H392MAR	801	F801RHK
248	F248NJN	256	F256RHK	304	H304LPU	393	H393MAR	802	F802RHK
249	F249NJN	257	F257RHK	305	H305LPU	394	H394MAR	803	F803RHK
250	F250NJN	258	F258RHK	306	H306LPU	395	H395MAR	804	F804RHK
251	F251NJN	259	F259RHK	388	H388MAR	396	K396KHJ		
252	F252NJN	260	F260RHK	389	H389MAR	397	K397KHJ		

805-811   **Mercedes-Benz 811D**   **Plaxton Beaver**

805	K805DJN	807	K807DJN	809	K809DJN	810	K810DJN	811	K811DJN
806	K806DJN	808	K808DJN						

411-419 Mercedes-Benz O810D Plaxton Beaver

411	R411VPU	413	R413VPU	415	R415VPU	417	R417VPU	419	R419VPU
412	R412VPU	414	R414VPU	416	R416VPU	418	R418VPU		

Note: These minibuses transferred to First Capital.

501-511 Optare Solo Optare

501	EO02FLA	504	EO02FLD	507	EO02FLG	509	EO02FLJ	511	EO02FKZ
502	EO02FLB	505	EO02FLE	508	EO02FLH	510	EO02FLK		
503	EO02FLC	506	EO02FLF						

Note: These Optare Solos transferred to First London along with route 193.

Epsom Buses

	R211MGT	Mercedes-Benz 0814D	UVG Citistar
	R212MGT	Mercedes-Benz 0814D	UVG Citistar
	R213MGT	Mercedes-Benz 0814D	UVG Citistar

MB15-9 Mercedes-Benz O814D Plaxton Beaver 2

MB15	S451LGN	MB16	S452LGN	MB17	S453LGN	MB18	S454LGN	MB19	S455LGN

OE1-11 Optare Solo Optare

OE 1	YE52FHH	OE 4	YE52FHL	OE 6	YE52FHN	OE 8	YE52FHP	OE10	YE52FHS
OE 2	YE52FHJ	OE 5	YE52FHM	OE 7	YE52FHO	OE 9	YE52FHR	OE11	YE52FHU
OE 3	YE52FHK								

OP12-21 Optare Solo Optare

OP12	YN03ZXF	OP15	YN53SVK	OP17	YN53SVO	OP19	YN53SVR	OP21	YN53ZXB
OP14	YN53SUF	OP16	YN53SVL	OP18	YN53SVP	OP20	YN53ZXA		

OP23-30 Optare Solo Optare

OP23	YJ09MHK	OP25	YJ09MHM	OP27	YJ09MHO	OP29	YJ09MHV	OP30	YJ09MHX
OP24	YJ09MHL	OP26	YJ09MHN	OP28	YJ09MHU				

OP31	YJ11EJA	Optare Solo	Optare
OP32	YJ11EJC	Optare Solo	Optare
OP33	YJ11EJD	Optare Solo	Optare
OP34	YJ13HJN	Optare Solo	Optare
OP35, 201	YJ14BGK	Optare Solo SR	Optare
OP36, 202	YJ14BGO	Optare Solo SR	Optare
	YJ14BGU	Optare Solo SR	Optare
	YJ14BGV	Optare Solo SR	Optare
	YJ66ARO	Optare Solo SR	Optare

OPL01-8 **Optare Solo SR** **Optare**

| OPL01 | YJ62FUD | OPL03 | YJ62FVN | OPL05 | YJ62FWB | OPL07 | YJ62FXG | OPL08 | YJ62FXK |
| OPL02 | YJ62FUG | OPL04 | YJ62FVT | OPL06 | YJ62FXA | | | | |

WS01-10 **Wrightbus Streetlite WF** **Wright**

| WS01 | SN64CTZ | WS03 | SN64CUH | WS05 | SN64CUU | WS07 | SN64CUW | WS09 | SN64CVB |
| WS02 | SN64CUA | WS04 | SN64CUK | WS06 | SN64CUV | WS08 | SN64CUY | WS10 | SN64CVC |

First London

MM1-10 **Mercedes-Benz 811D** **Marshall**

| MM 1 | N521REW | MM 3 | N523REW | MM 5 | N525REW | MM 7 | N527REW | MM 9 | P489CEG |
| MM 2 | N522REW | MM 4 | N524REW | MM 6 | N526REW | MM 8 | P488CEG | MM10 | P490CEG |

| MM25 | P825NAV | Mercedes-Benz Vario O814D | Marshall |
| MM26 | P826NAV | Mercedes-Benz Vario O814D | Marshall |

ML101-16 **Marshall Minibus** **Marshall**

ML101	R101VLX	ML105	R105VLX	ML109	R109VLX	ML113	R113VLX	ML115	R115VLX
ML102	R102VLX	ML106	R706VLX	ML110	R110VLX	ML114	R114VLX	ML116	R116VLX
ML103	R103VLX	ML107	R107VLX	ML111	R211VLX				
ML104	R104VLX	ML108	R108VLX	ML112	R112VLX				

ES797	LT02NVC	Mercedes-Benz Sprinter	Koch
ES798	LT02NVB	Mercedes-Benz Sprinter	Koch
ES799	LT02NVD	Mercedes-Benz Sprinter	Koch

OOS53701-6 **Optare Solo** **Optare**

| OOS53701 | LK05DYO | OOS53703 | LK05DXR | OOS53705 | LK05DXT | OOS53706 | LK05DXU |
| OOS53702 | LK05DXP | OOS53704 | LK05DXS | | | | |

Go-Ahead London

| OS1 | MX09HHW | Optare Solo | Optare |

ML1-15 **Marshall Minibus** **Marshall**

ML 1	P501HEG	ML 4	P504HEG	ML 7	P407KAV	ML10	P410KAV	ML13	P413KAV
ML 2	P502HEG	ML 5	P505HEG	ML 8	P408KAV	ML11	P411KAV	ML14	P404KAV
ML 3	P503HEG	ML 6	P506HEG	ML 9	P409KAV	ML12	P402KAV	ML15	P405KAV

MB1-8 Mercedes-Benz Sprinter City 45

MB 1	BT15KLZ	MB 3	BT66TZL	MB 5	BN17JFV	MB 7	BV19YKA	MB 8	BV19YKB
MB 2	BL16GAO	MB 4	BT66TZM	MB 6	BN17JFX				

WS1-9 Wrightbus Streetlite WF Wright

WS 1	LJ12CGF	WS 3	LJ12CGK	WS 5	LJ12CGU	WS 7	LJ12CGX	WS 9	LJ12CGZ
WS 2	LJ12CGG	WS 4	LJ12CGO	WS 6	LJ12CGV	WS 8	LJ12CGY		

WS33-48 Wrightbus Streetlite WF Wright

WS 33	SN64CTZ	WS 37	SN64CUH	WS 41	SN64CUU	WS 44	SN64CUX	WS 47	SN64CVB
WS 34	SN64CUA	WS 38	SN64CUJ	WS 42	SN64CUV	WS 45	SN64CUY	WS 48	SN64CVC
WS 35	SN64CUC	WS 39	SN64CUK	WS 43	SN64CUW	WS 46	SN64CVA		
WS 36	SN64CUG	WS 40	SN64CUO						

WS49-64 Wrightbus Streetlite WF Wright

WS49	SM15HWE	WS53	SM15HWJ	WS57	SM15VKB	WS60	SM15VKE	WS63	SM15WCN
WS50	SM15HWF	WS54	SM15HWK	WS58	SM15VKC	WS61	SM15WCK	WS64	SM15WCO
WS51	SM15HWG	WS55	SM15VJZ	WS59	SM15VKD	WS62	SM15WCL		
WS52	SM15HWH	WS56	SM15VKA						

WS79-86 Wrightbus Streetlite WF Wright

WS79	SK17HHE	WS81	SK17HKA	WS83	SK17HKC	WS85	SK17HKE	WS86	SK17HKF
WS80	SK17HHF	WS82	SK17HKB	WS84	SK17HKD				

Hackney Community Transport

OS2-8 Optare Solo Optare

OS2	YJ59NRN	OS4	YJ10EYF	OS6	YJ10EYH	OS7	YJ10EYK	OS8	YJ10EYL
OS3	YJ59NRO	OS5	YJ10EYG						

OS9-18 Optare Solo Optare

OS9	YJ60PFA	OS11	YJ60PFE	OS13	YJ60PFG	OS15	YJ60PFN	OS17	YJ60LRX
OS10	YJ60PFD	OS12	YJ60PFF	OS14	YJ60PFK	OS16	YJ60PFO	OS18	YJ60LRY

OS19-27 Optare Solo Optare

OS19	YJ61MKA	OS21	YJ12GVT	OS23	YJ12GVV	OS25	YJ12GVX	OS27	YJ12GVZ
OS20	YJ12GVR	OS22	YJ12GVU	OS24	YJ12GVW	OS26	YJ12GVY		

Harris/East Thames Buses

320-334 — Optare Excel — Optare

320	P320KAR	323	P323KAR	326	P326NHJ	329	P329NHJ	332	P332NHJ
321	P321KAR	324	P324NHJ	327	P327NHJ	330	P330NHJ	333	P333HBC
322	P322KAR	325	P325NHJ	328	P328NHJ	331	P331NHJ	334	P334NHJ

373-380 — Optare Excel — Optare

373	R373DJN	375	R375DJN	377	R377DJN	379	R379DJN	380	R380DJN
374	R374DJN	376	R376DJN	378	R378DJN				

Kentish Bus

804-890 — MCW MetroRider — MCW

804	E804BTN	809	E809BTN	861	F861LCU	864	F864LCU	889	H889OCU
807	E807BTN	810	E810BTN	862	F862LCU	865	F865LCU	890	H890OCU
808	E808BTN	860	F860LCU	863	F863LCU	887	H887OCU		

870-85 — Talbot Pullman — Talbot

870	G870SKE	874	G874SKE	878	G878SKE	881	G881SKE	884	G884SKE
871	G871SKE	875	G875SKE	879	G879SKE	882	G882SKE	885	G885SKE
872	G872SKE	876	G876SKE	880	G880SKE	883	G883SKE		
873	G873SKE	877	G877SKE						

London Northern/Metroline

MM254-78 — MAN 11.270 — Marshall

MM254	N121XEG	MM259	N126XEG	MM264	N131XEG	MM270	P470JEG	MM275	P475JEG
MM255	N122XEG	MM260	N127XEG	MM265	N132XEG	MM271	P471JEG	MM276	P476JEG
MM256	N123XEG	MM261	N128XEG	MM266	N133XEG	MM272	P472JEG	MM277	P477JEG
MM257	N124XEG	MM262	N129XEG	MM267	N134XEG	MM273	P473JEG	MM278	P478JEG
MM258	N125XEG	MM263	N130XEG	MM268	N135XEG	MM274	P474JEG		

MC1	P481HEG	Marshall Minibus	Marshall
MMS269	N161YEG	Mercedes-Benz 811D	Marshall
MRL223	P448SWX	Optare MetroRider	Optare
MRL224	P449SWX	Optare MetroRider	Optare
OM279	P509NWU	Optare MetroRider	Optare

NSM660-4 Optare Solo Optare

NSM660	YK05CCD	NSM662	YK05CCJ	NSM663	YK05CCN	NSM664	YK05CCO
NSM661	YK05CCE						

OS2499-2504 Optare Solo SR Optare

OSE2750

OS2499	YJ68FXA	OS2501	YJ68FXF	OS2503	YJ68FXE	OSE2750	OP02ARE
OS2500	YJ68FXB	OS2502	YJ68FXC	OS2504	YJ68FXG		

Metrobus

121-8 Mercedes-Benz 709D Reeve Burgess

121	F121TRU	123	F123TRU	125	F125TRU	127	F127TRU	128	F128TRU
122	F122TRU	124	F124TRU	126	F126TRU				

Optare MetroRider Optare

	N901HWY		N903HWY		N904HWY		N905HWY		N906HWY
	N902HWY								

501-10 Optare Excel Optare

501	P501OUG	503	P503OUG	505	P505OUG	507	P507OUG	509	P509OUG
502	P502OUG	504	P504OUG	506	P506OUG	508	P508OUG	510	P510OUG

101	YJ56WVF	Optare Solo	Optare
102	YJ56WVG	Optare Solo	Optare
396	LW52AFA	Optare Solo	Optare

Mitcham Belle

Optare Solo Optare

	KX51UCS		KX51UCT	KX51UCU		KX51UCV

R&I Tours

Iveco 49.10 Robin Hood

	F201HGN		F204HGN		F207HGN		F209HGN	G211LGK
	F202HGN		F205HGN		F208HGN		F210HGN	G212LGK
	F203HGN		F206HGN					

243	M501ALP	Optare Metrorider	Optare
244	M502ALP	Optare Metrorider	Optare

RATP London

WS1	SN65OKM	Wright Streetlite WF	Wright

MS75091-100   **MAN TGE**

M75091	OV69DXU	M75093	OV69DXC	M75095	OV69DXM	M75097	OV69DWG	M75099	OV69DWJ
M75092	OV69DWK	M75094	OV69DYN	M75096	OU69XPJ	M75098	OV69DVX	M75100	OV69DVZ

Sovereign, Harrow

403-424   **Mercedes-Benz 811D**   **Reeve Burgess Beaver**

403	H403FGS	408	H408FGS	413	H413FGS	419	H419FGS	423	H423FGS
404	H404FGS	409	H409FGS	415	H415FGS	421	H421FGS	424	H424FGS
406	H406FGS	410	H410FGS	417	H417FGS	422	H422FGS		
407	H407FGS	411	H411FGS	418	H418FGS				

920-931   **Mercedes-Benz 709D**   **Reeve Burgess Beaver**

920	H920FGS	922	H922FGS	925	H925FGS	927	H927FGS	930	H930FGS
921	H921FGS	923	H923FGS	926	H926FGS	929	H929FGS	931	H931FGS

Stagecoach London

453-1311   **Volvo B6**   **Alexander Dash**

453	M453VHE	457	M457VHE	1303	M743PRS	1306	M746PRS	1309	M749PRS
454	M454VHE	458	M458VHE	1304	M744PRS	1307	M847PRS	1310	M750PRS
455	M455VHE	1301	M741PRS	1305	M745PRS	1308	M748PRS	1311	M846HDF
456	M456VHE	1302	M742PRS						

MB1-18   **Mercedes-Benz Vario O814D**   **Plaxton Beaver 2**

MB 1	R501YWC	MB 6	R506YWC	MB11	R511YWC	MB16	R516YWC
MB 2	R502YWC	MB 7	R507YWC	MB12	R512YWC	MB17	R517YWC
MB 3	R503YWC	MB 8	R508YWC	MB13	R513YWC	MB18	R518YWC
MB 4	R504YWC	MB 9	R509YWC	MB14	R514YWC		
MB 5	R505YWC	MB10	R510YWC	MB15	R515YWC		

Sullivan Buses

SL90-8 **Wrightbus Streetlite DF** **Wright**

| SL90 | CP67SUL | SL92 | JJ67SUL | SL94 | LW67SUL | SL96 | PJ67SUL | SL98 | SL15ZGR |
| SL91 | JF67SUL | SL93 | KT67SUL | SL95 | MH67SUL | SL97 | SL67SUL | | |

Transcity

Talbot Pullman **Talbot**

| | F814AVC | | G133AHP | | G213AHP | | G214AHP | | G640BHP |

Travel London

Optare Excel **Optare**

	R401HWU		R407HWU		R411HWU		R415HWU		R419HWU
	R402HWU		R408HWU		R412HWU		R416HWU		R420HWU
	R403HWU		R409HWU		R413HWU		R417HWU		R421HWU
	R404HWU		R410HWU		R414HWU		R418HWU		R422HWU
	R405HWU								

Optare Solo **Optare**

| | S231EWU | | S233EWU | | S235EWU | | S237EWU | | S239EWU |
| | S232EWU | | S234EWU | | S236EWU | | S238EWU | | S240EWU |

Uno

| 46 | SN64CVA | Wrightbus Streetlite WF | Wright |

Appendix II
EARLY SMALL BUSES

Fleet No.	Reg. No.	Chassis	Body	New to
MS 1	AKJ872	Morris YB6	Duple	Grey Motor Coach Services, Longfield
MS 2	HA7041	Morris YB6	Holbrook	Morris Motors (Demonstrator)
MS 3	JH2585	Morris YB6	Duple	Lewis Omnibus Co., Watford
MS 4	PL6461	Morris YB6	Weymann	East Surrey Traction Company
MS 5	PL6462	Morris YB6	Weymann	East Surrey Traction Company
MS 6	PL6463	Morris YB6	Weymann	East Surrey Traction Company
MS 7	PL6464	Morris YB6	Weymann	East Surrey Traction Company
MS 8	PL6465	Morris YB6	Weymann	East Surrey Traction Company
MS 9	PL6466	Morris YB6	Weymann	East Surrey Traction Company
MS10	PL6459	Morris YB6	Harrington	East Surrey Traction Company
MS11	PL6460	Morris YB6	Harrington	East Surrey Traction Company
	PF1198	Morris 1 ton		H T Molyneaux, Bletchingley
	KX3813	Morris 30cwt	Markham	Borough Bus, Windsor
	KX3814	Morris 30cwt	Markham	Borough Bus, Windsor
	RX5736	Morris	Duple	Hewins Garage, Maidenhead
	RX3459	Morris Z6		W F Clatworthy, Windsor
	RX5232	Morris Commercial TX	Reall	Crescent Coaches, Windsor
	RX5634	Morris Commercial TX	Reall	Cream Service, Slough
	RX9603	Morris Commercial TX	Reall	Cream Service, Slough
	UU5009	Morris R	Buckingham	Great Western Railway
	VX9932	Morris Commercial Dictator	Metcalfe	Imperial Bus Service, Romford
NY 1	JH492	Thornycroft A12	Thurgood	People's Motor Services, Ware
NY 2	JH1586	Thornycroft A12	Thurgood	People's Motor Services, Ware
NY 3	JH2054	Thornycroft A12	Thurgood	People's Motor Services, Ware
NY 4	UR7141	Thornycroft A2L	Thurgood	People's Motor Services, Ware
NY 5	UR7142	Thornycroft A2L	Thurgood	People's Motor Services, Ware
NY 6	UR7353	Thornycroft A2L	Thurgood	People's Motor Services, Ware
NY 7	UR7736	Thornycroft A2L	Thurgood	People's Motor Services, Ware
NY 8	UR7968	Thornycroft A2L	Thurgood	People's Motor Services, Ware
NY 9	UR9176	Thornycroft A2L	Thurgood	People's Motor Services, Ware
	PG1099	Thornycroft A2L	Challands Ross	Woking & District
	PG2018	Thornycroft A2L	Challands Ross	Woking & District

Fleet No.	Reg. No.	Chassis	Body	New to
	PG3236	Thornycroft A2L	Challands Ross	Woking & District
	PG4226	Thornycroft A2L	Challands Ross	Woking & District
	VB4550	Thornycroft A2L	Wilton	Woking & District
	KO9092	Thornycroft A2L	Vincent	West Kent Motor Services
	EKP140	Thornycroft Dainty	Thurgood	West Kent Motor Services
TH1	UV4086	Thornycroft BC	Vickers	Great Western Railway
TH2	UV4087	Thornycroft BC	Vickers	Great Western Railway
TH3	UV4088	Thornycroft BC	Vickers	Great Western Railway
	PG1757	Thornycroft BC	Challands Ross	Woking & District
	PG1758	Thornycroft BC	Challands Ross	Woking & District
	OT7822	Thornycroft LB		Woking & District
	JH1587	Thornycroft Cygnet	Thurgood	People's Motor Services, Ware
	JH3338	Thornycroft Cygnet	Thurgood	People's Motor Services, Ware
	JH3432	Thornycroft Cygnet	Thurgood	People's Motor Services, Ware
	TW8532	Chevrolet LM	Metcalfe	Romford & District
	YU9022	Chevrolet LM	Thurgood	A E Blane (Imperial), Romford
	KO6155	Chevrolet LM		Penfolrd & Brodie
	RO8517	Chevrolet LM	Thurgood	People's Bus, Ware
	PH6509	Chevrolet LM		A R Rudall (Magnet), Guildford
	UC6438	Chevrolet LM		Carr & Hollings, Hemel Hempstead
	KX1343	Chevrolet LP	Hoyal	A H Lucas, Slough
5	KX1580	Chevrolet LP	Willmott	Amersham & District
	KX3075	Chevrolet LQ		Bell's Bus Service, Slough
	PK6935	Chevrolet LQ		R G Heywood, Weybridge
	UR3273	Chevrolet LQ		A E Gilbert, Essendon
	UR4218	Chevrolet LQ		R J Allery, Abbots Langley
	UV9957	Chevrolet LQ		Youens, Watford
	UW7614	Chevrolet LQ		Clark's Motor Coaches
	UW6727	Chevrolet LQ		Bell's Bus Service, Slough
	KX4076	Chevrolet LQ		TT Bus Service, Slough
	KX4530	Chevrolet LQ		Wycombe & District
	KX4534	Chevrolet LQ		F H Evans & Son, High Wycombe
	GC5531	Chevrolet LQ		Barton, Watford
	MY6839	Chevrolet LQ		Edwards Motor Service, Rainham
	PG7703	Chevrolet LQ		Magnet Omnibus Service, Guildford
	PG9110	Chevrolet LQ		The Egham Motor Co.
	VX4074	Chevrolet LQ	Furber	Regent, Brentwood
	GK9584	Chevrolet U		Bell's Bus Service, Slough
	GJ3757	Chevrolet U	Willowbrook	Bell's Bus Service, Slough
	HX9676	Chevrolet U	Reall	Bell's Bus Service, Slough
	HX9677	Chevrolet U	Reall	F Berry, Slough

Fleet No.	Reg. No.	Chassis	Body	New to
	KX5977	Chevrolet U		F S Bowler, Beaconsfield
	RX7545	Chevrolet U	Hoyal	A H Lucas, Slough
	KX6513	Chevrolet U		Chesham & District
	GO9046	Chevrolet U	Thurgood	Chesham & District
	KX7490	Chevrolet U	Willmott	A H Lucas, Slough
	PL1211	Chevrolet U		H Cooke, Weybridge
	RX7617	Chevrolet U		Speedwell Bus Service, Windsor
	KO3306	Willy-Overland-Crossley Manchester		Gravesend & District Bus Services
	VX8540	Willy-Overland-Crossley Manchester		Tilbury Dock Coaches
	KR6859	Willy-Overland-Crossley Manchester		Gravesend & District Bus Services
	KJ4016	Willy-Overland-Crossley Manchester		Gravesend & District Bus Services
	KJ4191	Willy-Overland-Crossley Manchester		Gravesend & District Bus Services
	KR3034	Willy-Overland-Crossley Manchester		Gravesend & District Bus Services
	KR7090	Willy-Overland-Crossley Manchester		Gravesend & District Bus Services
BN 1	MV933	Bean	Birch	Royal Highlander
BN 2	HX3466	Bean	Birch	Royal Highlander
BN 3	HX3467	Bean	Birch	Royal Highlander
BN 4	MY3496	Bean	Birch	The Pinner Bus
BN 5	DV5364	Bean	Tiverton Coachworks	W A Hart, Budleigh Salterton, Devon
	YN4594	Bean		H A Turner, Wandsworth
	UL1771	Bean	Birch	H A Turner, Wandsworth
	RF5806	Bean		East Surrey Buses
	KP4275	Bean		C H Hever (Darneth Bus Service)
	KO8824	Bean		C H Hever (Darneth Bus Service)
	KO9958	Bean		C H Hever (Darneth Bus Service)
	YX7518	Bean		C H Hever (Darneth Bus Service)
	GJ3390	Bean		Sevenoaks Motor Services
	GJ5077	Bean		Sevenoaks Motor Services
	UR6278	Bean	Thurgood	St Albans & District
	UR6279	Bean	Thurgood	St Albans & District
	KX4018	Bean		F Berry, Slough
	RX7554	Bean	Duple	F C Owens, Slough
	EV2060	Bean	Strachan	Stephen's Rainham Bus Services
DM 1	VA4584	Dennis 30cwt	Strachan	Romford & District

Fleet No.	Reg. No.	Chassis	Body	New to
DM 2	EV4010	Dennis 30cwt	Metcalfe	Romford & District
DM 3	GJ2307	Dennis GL	Duple	Romford & District
DM 4	VX9897	Dennis GL	Duple	Romford & District
DM 5	VX3180	Dennis G	Metcalfe	Imperial, Romford
DM 6	VX6739	Dennis 30cwt	Thurgood	Imperial, Romford
DM 7	VX7401	Dennis 30cwt	Metcalfe	Imperial, Romford
DM 8	VX7354	Dennis 30cwt	Thurgood	Imperial, Romford
	KO6137	Dennis 30cwt	Vickers	West Kent Motor Services, Dunton Green
D203	KO6244	Dennis 30cwt	Vickers	West Kent Motor Services, Dunton Green
	KO7272	Dennis G	Strachan & Brown	West Kent Motor Services, Dunton Green
	KO8017	Dennis G	Wilton	West Kent Motor Services, Dunton Green
D202	KR5018	Dennis 30cwt	Short	Edward's Motor Services
	DY4622	Dennis 30cwt		Armstrong & Stratton, St Leonards
	KP59	Dennis 30cwt		Gravesend & District Bus Services Ltd
	KP1587	Dennis 30cwt		Gravesend & District Bus Services Ltd
	KP3796	Dennis G		Gravesend & District Bus Services Ltd
	KP4951	Dennis G		Gravesend & District Bus Services Ltd
	KP7159	Dennis G		Gravesend & District Bus Services Ltd
	KR438	Dennis G		Gravesend & District Bus Services Ltd
	KR705	Dennis G		Gravesend & District Bus Services Ltd
	PG3194	Dennis 30cwt		W Eggleton Ltd, Woking
	PG8716	Dennis 30cwt		W Eggleton Ltd, Woking
	PH5276	Dennis 30cwt		W Eggleton Ltd, Woking
	PL5896	Dennis GL		W Eggleton Ltd, Woking
	PG7438	Dennis GL		W Eggleton Ltd, Woking
	OT8598	Dennis G	Strachan & Brown	Aldershot & District Traction Co. Ltd
	GU7544	Dennis 30cwt		R J Robson, Cookham
	XV6303	Dennis G		Howe's Brown Bus, Englefield Green
	PP7700	Dennis 30cwt	Strachan	Amersham & District
	KX1326	Dennis G	Strachan	Amersham & District
	KX5923	Dennis GL	Strachan	Amersham & District
	KX5967	Dennis GL	Strachan	Amersham & District
	KX8569	Dennis GL	Strachan	Amersham & District
	VX6341	Dennis GL	Thurgood	Edward's Motor Services
	VW6182	Dennis G		The Reliable Omnibus & Motor Coaches
	VW7400	Dennis G		The Reliable Omnibus & Motor Coaches
	GC1313	Dennis 30cwt	Wilmott	The Reliable Omnibus & Motor Coaches
	GP5047	Dennis GL		The Reliable Omnibus & Motor Coaches
DC1	AKR937	Dennis Ace		London Passenger Transport Board

Fleet No.	Reg. No.	Chassis	Body	New to
DC2	BPF493	Dennis Ace	Waveney	London Passenger Transport Board
DC3	BBH755	Dennis Ace		Penn Bus Co., High Wycombe
	CKL719	Dennis Ace		West Kent Motor Services, Dunton Green
	CPF349	Dennis Ace		Walton-on-Thames Bus Co.
	DPD859	Dennis Ace		Aldershot & District Traction Co. Ltd
	EPK29	Dennis Ace		Aldershot & District Traction Co. Ltd
	JB4838	Dennis Ace		White Bus Service, Winkfield
	JB9468	Dennis Ace		White Bus Service, Winkfield
DA 1	GF494	Dennis Dart	Chiswick	London General Omnibus Company
DA 2	GF493	Dennis Dart	Chiswick	London General Omnibus Company
DA 3	GF492	Dennis Dart	Chiswick	London General Omnibus Company
DA 4	GF491	Dennis Dart	Chiswick	London General Omnibus Company
DA 5	GF7207	Dennis Dart	Chiswick	London General Omnibus Company
DA 6	GF7216	Dennis Dart	Chiswick	London General Omnibus Company
DA 7	GH8078	Dennis Dart	Chiswick	London General Omnibus Company
DA 8	GH8079	Dennis Dart	Chiswick	London General Omnibus Company
DA 9	GH8080	Dennis Dart	Chiswick	London General Omnibus Company
DA10	GH8081	Dennis Dart	Chiswick	London General Omnibus Company
DA11	GH8082	Dennis Dart	Chiswick	London General Omnibus Company
DA12	GK3049	Dennis Dart	Chiswick	London General Omnibus Company
DA13	GK3050	Dennis Dart	Chiswick	London General Omnibus Company
DA14	GK3070	Dennis Dart	Chiswick	London General Omnibus Company
DA15	GK3075	Dennis Dart	Chiswick	London General Omnibus Company
DA16	GK3090	Dennis Dart	Chiswick	London General Omnibus Company
DA17	GK3100	Dennis Dart	Chiswick	London General Omnibus Company
DA18	GK3101	Dennis Dart	Chiswick	London General Omnibus Company
DA19	GK3108	Dennis Dart	Chiswick	London General Omnibus Company
DA20	GK3132	Dennis Dart	Chiswick	London General Omnibus Company
DA21	GK5342	Dennis Dart	Chiswick	London General Omnibus Company
DA22	GK5441	Dennis Dart	Chiswick	London General Omnibus Company
DA23	GK5442	Dennis Dart	Chiswick	London General Omnibus Company
DA24	GN2145	Dennis Dart	Chiswick	London General Omnibus Company
DA25	GN2146	Dennis Dart	Chiswick	London General Omnibus Company
DA26	GN4738	Dennis Dart	Chiswick	London General Omnibus Company
DA27	GN4739	Dennis Dart	Chiswick	London General Omnibus Company
DA28	GN4740	Dennis Dart	Chiswick	London General Omnibus Company
DA29	GN4741	Dennis Dart	Chiswick	London General Omnibus Company
DA30	GN4742	Dennis Dart	Chiswick	London General Omnibus Company
DA31	GO618	Dennis Dart	Chiswick	London General Omnibus Company
DA32	GO661	Dennis Dart	Chiswick	London General Omnibus Company

Fleet No.	Reg. No.	Chassis	Body	New to
DA33	GX5325	Dennis Dart	Chiswick	London General Omnibus Company
DA34	GX5326	Dennis Dart	Chiswick	London General Omnibus Company
DA35	GX5331	Dennis Dart	Chiswick	London General Omnibus Company
DA36	GX5327	Dennis Dart	Chiswick	London General Omnibus Company
DA37	GX5332	Dennis Dart	Chiswick	London General Omnibus Company
DA38	GX5333	Dennis Dart	Chiswick	London General Omnibus Company
DA39	JJ4333	Dennis Dart	Chiswick	London General Omnibus Company
DA40	JJ4334	Dennis Dart	Chiswick	London General Omnibus Company
DA41	JJ4373	Dennis Dart	Chiswick	London General Omnibus Company
DA42	JJ4374	Dennis Dart	Chiswick	London General Omnibus Company
DA43	EV4011	Dennis Dart	Metcalfe	Romford & District
DA44	EV5909	Dennis Dart	Metcalfe	Romford & District
DA45	ANO794	Dennis Dart	Metcalfe	Romford & District
BD 1	AGY485	Bedford WLB		Greenhithe & District Bus Services
BD 2	AHK434	Bedford WLB	Strachan	The Reliable Bus Service, South Stifford
BD 3	AKE725	Bedford WLB	Duple	Greenhithe & District Bus Services
BD 4	AKK458	Bedford WLB	Duple	Gravesend & District Bus Services
BD 5	AKM308	Bedford WLB		Enterprise Gravesend
BD 6	AMF595	Bedford WLB	Duple	Warwick, Farnham Common
BD 7	AMH881	Bedford WLB	Duple	Warwick, Farnham Common
BD 8	AMY660	Bedford WLB	Reall	Purfleet Bus Service
BD 9	APB940	Bedford WLB	Duple	The Egham Motor Co.
BD10	APC55	Bedford WLB	Duple	Sunshine Saloon Coaches, Kingston
BD11	EV8977	Bedford WLB	Duple	Harvey's Transport, West Thurrock
BD12	EV8978	Bedford WLB	Duple	Harvey's Transport, West Thurrock
BD13	JH550	Bedford WLB	Strachan	Albanian Bus Co.
BD14	JH911	Bedford WLB	Strachan	Albanian Bus Co.
BD15	JH974	Bedford WLB	Duple	Express Motor Service, St Albans
BD16	JH1300	Bedford WLB		Victoria Omnibus Service, St Albans
BD17	JH2314	Bedford WLB	Thurgood	Reliance Coaches, St Albans
BD18	KJ4255	Bedford WLB		The Enterprise Motor Service, Gravesend
BD19	KJ4256	Bedford WLB		The Enterprise Motor Service, Gravesend
BD20	MV6324	Bedford WLB	Duple	Bluebell Services, Stanwell
BD21	PJ1727	Bedford WLB		T Harwood, Weybridge
BD22	PJ1806	Bedford WLB		J H Burgess, Englefield Green
BD23	PJ8430	Bedford WLB	Wycombe	G F Gorringe, Kingston-upon-Thames
	KX7894	Bedford WHG		Berry, Slough
	JH238	Bedford WLB	Thurgood	Berkhamsted & District
	JH2313	Bedford WLB	Thurgood	Albanian Bus Co.
	JH5324	Bedford WLB	Thurgood	Berkhamsted & District

C1-113 Leyland Cub

C 1	AYV717	C 23	BXD648	C 45	BXD670	C 67	BXD692	C 89	CLE117
C 2	BXD631	C 24	BXD649	C 46	BXD671	C 68	BXD693	C 90	CLE118
C 3	BXD627	C 25	BXD650	C 47	BXD672	C 69	BXD694	C 91	CLE119
C 4	BXD628	C 26	BXD651	C 48	BXD673	C 70	BXD695	C 92	CLE120
C 5	BXD629	C 27	BXD652	C 49	BXD674	C 71	BXD696	C 93	CLE121
C 6	BXD632	C 28	BXD653	C 50	BXD675	C 72	BXD697	C 94	CLE122
C 7	BXD630	C 29	BXD654	C 51	BXD676	C 73	BXD698	C 95	CLE123
C 8	BXD633	C 30	BXD655	C 52	BXD677	C 74	BXD699	C 96	CLE124
C 9	BXD634	C 31	BXD656	C 53	BXD678	C 75	BXD700	C 97	CLE125
C 10	BXD635	C 32	BXD657	C 54	BXD679	C 76	JH2401	C 98	CLE126
C 11	BXD636	C 33	BXD658	C 55	BXD680	C 77	CLE105	C106	CLX543
C 12	BXD637	C 34	BXD659	C 56	BXD681	C 78	CLE106	C107	CLX544
C 13	BXD638	C 35	BXD660	C 57	BXD682	C 79	CLE107	C108	CLX545
C 14	BXD639	C 36	BXD661	C 58	BXD683	C 80	CLE108	C109	CLX546
C 15	BXD640	C 37	BXD662	C 59	BXD684	C 81	CLE109	C110	CLX547
C 16	BXD641	C 38	BXD663	C 60	BXD685	C 82	CLE110	C111	CLX548
C 17	BXD642	C 39	BXD664	C 61	BXD686	C 83	CLE111	C112	CLX549
C 18	BXD643	C 40	BXD665	C 62	BXD687	C 84	CLE112	C113	CLX550
C 19	BXD644	C 41	BXD666	C 63	BXD688	C 85	CLE113		
C 20	BXD645	C 42	BXD667	C 64	BXD689	C 86	CLE114		
C 21	BXD646	C 43	BXD668	C 65	BXD690	C 87	CLE115		
C 22	BXD647	C 44	BXD669	C 66	BXD691	C 88	CLE116		

C1 was bodied by LPTB; C2-75 were bodied by Short Bros.; C76 carried bodywork by an unknown builder.
C77-98 were bodied by Weymann; C106-13 were bodied by Park Royal.

Sources

Glazier, Ken, *London Bus File 1933-35,* Capital Transport, 2002
Lane, Kevin, *An Illustrated History of London Buses,* Ian Allan, 1997
London Omnibus Traction Society, *The London Bus,* Various issues

Websites
Ian's Bus Stop, www.countrybus.org
www.londonbuses.co.uk